Early Praise for *Adrenaline Ju*

CW01083101

"Brilliantly insightful. At one moment
we're toast' followed quickly by the rea:
There's hope!'" —**Howard Look**, VP,

"Who else but these particular authors
team experience to capture memorable names for oft-encountered situations? I suspect you will start using these phrases in your work—I already
have." —**Alistair Cockburn**, author of *Agile Software Development*

"The 86 project patterns are grimly familiar to anyone who has worked
in project-related organizations. Fortunately, some of the patterns are
good ones, and should be encouraged. Sadly, though, many of the
others are not only depressingly familiar, but astonishingly destructive to
productivity, quality, and the morale of the project team."
—**Ed Yourdon**, author of *Death March*

"Written with a combined sense of humor and deep insight. The book
clearly conveys why projects fail and what can be done about it. It is all
doable practical advice delivered in a very friendly and acceptable way."
—**Warren McFarland**, Professor, Harvard Business School

"This is an absolutely must-read book for everyone running an IT
organization. Actually, the lessons in this wonderful book are applicable
to anyone running any kind of project-based organization—just about
every organization. The metaphors are funny in that kind of tragic-
funny *you've been there* kind of way. You will recognize the common
pathologies of projects everywhere. With a dose of courage and this
book in hand, you will be able to create a healthy project environment
where people can thrive and still deliver consistent results."
—**Lynne Ellyn**, Sr. Vice President and CIO, DTE Energy

"People have always tried to understand themselves and each other. Our
survival has depended on such understanding, as has the quality of that
survival, from bare subsistence to deeply fulfilling livelihood. What
people do individually, interpersonally, and within their institutional
matrices, forms distinct frameworks of attitude and behavior. Perceiving
the dynamics of these complexes (let's call them) confers both insight and
power. Three attempts at such understanding leap to mind. The Chinese
had the *I Ching,* or *Book of Changes.* Architects have had *A Pattern Language.* And medical psychology has had its *Diagnostic and Statistical Manual
of Mental Disorders.* Brilliantly blending elements of all three (not least
from that last one), *Adrenaline Junkies and Template Zombies* maps the patterns people create and follow—to their detriment and advantage—in
the projects they engage within organizational contexts. Sharp, funny
and dead-on-target, the book deserves a wide reading."
—**Christopher Locke**, coauthor of *The Cluetrain Manifesto*

Also Available from Dorset House Publishing

Agile Software Development in the Large:
Diving Into the Deep
by Jutta Eckstein
ISBN: 978-0-932633-57-6   Copyright ©2004   248 pages, softcover

Becoming a Technical Leader:
An Organic Problem-Solving Approach
by Gerald M. Weinberg
ISBN: 978-0-932633-02-6   Copyright ©1986   304 pages, softcover

The Deadline: A Novel About Project Management
by Tom DeMarco
ISBN: 978-0-932633-39-2   Copyright ©1997   320 pages, softcover

Hiring the Best Knowledge Workers, Techies & Nerds:
The Secrets & Science of Hiring Technical People
by Johanna Rothman
ISBN: 978-0-932633-59-0   Copyright ©2004   352 pages, softcover

Peopleware: Productive Projects and Teams, 2nd ed.
by Tom DeMarco and Timothy Lister
ISBN: 978-0-932633-43-9   Copyright ©1999   264 pages, softcover

Waltzing With Bears: Managing Risk on Software Projects
by Tom DeMarco and Timothy Lister
ISBN: 978-0-932633-60-6   Copyright ©2003   208 pages, softcover

Working Up to Project Management: How Crushing Rocks at the
Asphalt Plant Prepared Me for Government Work
by Dwayne Phillips
ISBN: 978-0-932633-66-8   Copyright ©2008   216 pages, softcover

---

For More Information

✔ Contact us for prices, shipping options, availability, and more.

✔ Sign up to receive *INSIDE DORSET HOUSE (iDH)* by mail or fax.

✔ Send e-mail to subscribe to *iDH,* our e-mail newsletter.

✔ Visit Dorsethouse.com for savings, reviews, downloads, and more.

DORSET HOUSE PUBLISHING
An Independent Publisher of Books on
Systems and Software Development and Management. Since 1984.
353 West 12th Street   New York, NY 10014   USA
1-800-DH-BOOKS   1-800-342-6657
212-620-4053   fax: 212-727-1044
info@dorsethouse.com   www.dorsethouse.com

Adrenaline Junkies and Template Zombies

Understanding Patterns of Project Behavior

Tom DeMarco, Peter Hruschka
Tim Lister, Steve McMenamin
James Robertson, Suzanne Robertson

Dorset House Publishing
353 West 12th Street
New York, NY 10014

www.dorsethouse.com

Library of Congress Cataloging-in-Publication Data

Adrenaline junkies and template zombies : understanding patterns of project
behavior / Tom DeMarco ... [et al.].
    p. cm.
  ISBN 978-0-932633-67-5
1. Organizational behavior. 2. Corporate culture. 3. Management. 4. Employee
motivation. I. DeMarco, Tom.

HD58.7.D444 2008
302.3'5--dc22
                    2008000865

Quantity discounts are available from the publisher. Call (800) 342-6657 or (212) 620-4053 or e-mail info@dorsethouse.com. Contact same for examination copy requirements and permissions. To photocopy passages for academic use, obtain permission from the Copyright Clearance Center: (978) 750-8400 or www.copyright.com.

Trademark credits: All trade and product names are either trademarks, registered trademarks, or service marks of their respective companies, and are the property of their respective holders and should be treated as such.

The authors and the publisher have taken care in the preparation of this book, but make no express or implied warranty of any kind and assume no responsibility for errors or omissions. No liability is assumed for incidental or consequential damages in connection with or arising out of the use of the information or programs contained herein.

Cover and Interior Design: James Robertson

Distributed in the English language in Singapore, the Philippines, and Southeast Asia by Alkem Company (S) Pte. Ltd., Singapore; and in the English language in India, Bangladesh, Sri Lanka, Nepal, and Mauritius by Prism Books Pvt., Ltd., Bangalore, India.

Printed in the United States of America

Library of Congress Catalog Number: 2008000865

ISBN-13: 978-0-932633-67-5

            12 11 10 9 8 7 6 5 4 3 2

Contents

Introduction 3

1 Adrenaline Junkies................................6

2 Rattle Yer Dags 9

3 Dead Fish 12

4 Happy Clappy Meetings 14

5 Nanny 16

6 Referred Pain 19

7 Mañana 22

8 Eye Contact 25

9 Management By Mood Ring.................28

10 True Believer 32

11 Lease Your Soul..............................34

12 System Development Lemming Cycle.................36

13 No Bench 38

14 Face Time......................................40

15 I Gave You a Chisel. Why Aren't You
    Michelangelo? 43

16 Dashboards 45

17 Endless Huddle..............................49

18 Young Pups and Old Dogs................52

19 Film Critics 55

20 One Throat to Choke......................58

Interlude: Project-Speak 61

21 Soviet Style..................................63

22 Natural Authority 66

23 The Too-Quiet Office.....................68

24 The White Line.............................69

25 Silence Gives Consent....................72

26 Straw Man...................................74

27 Counterfeit Urgency......................77

28 Time Removes Cards from Your Hand.................79

29 Lewis & Clark...............................82

Contents

30 Short Pencil 85

31 Rhythm 87

32 The Overtime Predictor 89

33 Poker Night 92

34 False Quality Gates 95

35 Testing Before Testing 99

36 Cider House Rules 101

37 Talk Then Write 104

38 Project Sluts..107

39 Atlas..109

40 Everyone Wears Clothes for a Reason 112

41 Peer Preview 114

42 Snorkeling and Scuba Diving 117

43 It's Always the Goddamned Interfaces..............120

44 The Blue Zone 122

45 News Improvement 124

46 Telling the Truth Slowly..................................127

47 Practicing Endgame 130

48 The Music Makers 133

49 Journalists 136

50 The Empty Chair 138

51 My Cousin Vinny 140

52 Feature Soup..143

53 Data Qualty 146

54 Ben 148

55 Miss Manners 150

56 Undivided Attention 152

57 "There's No Crying in Baseball!" 155

58 Cool Hand Luke 157

59 Shipping On-Time, Every Time 159

60 Food++ 161

61 Orphaned Deliverables...163

62 Hidden Beauty 166

63 I Don't Know..169

64 Children of Lake Wobegon 172

65 Co-Education...176

66 Seelenverwandtschaft 179

67 Phillips Head 182

68 Predicting Innovation 184

69 Marilyn Munster 187

Interlude: The Cutting Room Floor......................190

70 Brownie in Motion 192

71 Loud and Clear..194

72 Safety Valve...197

73 Babel...200

74 Surprise! 202

75 Fridge Door 204

76 The Sun'll Come Out Tomorrow 207

77 Piling On...211

78 Seasons for Change 213

79 Paper Mill...216

80 Offshore Follies...218

81 War Rooms 221

82 What Smell?..223

83 Lessons Unlearned 225

84 Sanctity of the Half-Baked Idea.....................228

85 Leakage 230

86 Template Zombies...233

Photo Credits 235

Pattern Index 237

About the Guild..240

Adrenaline Junkies and Template Zombies

Understanding Patterns of Project Behavior

Introduction

Abstraction is uniquely human. It is something we do every day, every waking hour. But it wasn't always so. At some point in our prehistory, there had to be a very first instance of abstraction, a moment when an early protohuman stared at something vaguely familiar, and then with a sudden flash of insight, thought, "Hello! Thingumbob again!" That was the first abstraction. From that moment on, everything was different. Man was loose on the Earth.

Abstraction is profoundly human, but pattern recognition is not. It is not unique to humans at all. The mouse has figured out when the cat is likely to be asleep, when the humans are sure to be out of the kitchen, and when the crumbs have been recently dropped but not yet swept up. Your family dog knows all the signals that precede what *you* thought was going to be a totally unexpected getaway weekend. (Could it have been the suitcase?) And the neighborhood raccoon understands that when the tide is out, pickings are bound to be better on the beach than  in your compost pile. But for all their pattern recognition mastery, what the mouse/dog/raccoon cannot do is observe, "Hello! Thingumbob again!"[1] That involves abstraction.

The key difference is how the essence is captured. Patterns are absorbed and refined over time, stored away in the deep, nonverbal recesses of your mind, and conveyed to you in the form of hunches. The hunch that a particular ballcarrier is about to dart left, or that your

---

[1] The thingumbob quote is adapted from William James, *The Principles of Psychology* (New York: Henry Holt and Company, 1890), p. 463.

3

spouse is ready to explode in anger, is the result of recognized patterns from the past. So is the hunch that this week's project status meeting is going to be contentious. The unarticulated pattern may be useful to you—it clearly has survival value—but its value can increase markedly when you mull it over and begin to develop from it some declarable observations.

For example, ask yourself this question: What did the few contentious meetings over the past year all have in common? *Well, they were most often the ones that the boss's boss attended, usually near the end of a quarter. In the worst meetings, the team reported a slip in the schedule.* You form this into a statement of the pattern: "My boss tends to be extremely cranky about slip reported at a meeting, especially near the end of the quarter, when his own boss is in attendance."

The recognized signals that led to this observation are still buried in your unconscious, still able to provide you with occasional hunches. But now, in a momentary connection between the right brain hunch and the left brain articulation capability, you've isolated the essence and turned it into words. You can write it down, formulate tests to check its validity, share it with others, and merge your observations with those of your coworkers.

Most people who do project work are pretty good at pattern recognition and derived hunches ("I sense that this project is headed for disaster"), but not so good at abstracting their patterns into a more usable form. Thus this book. We six authors have put our heads together to articulate the patterns we've been absorbing during our combined one hundred and fifty years of experience.

The form of a book imposes a certain ordering of presentation, since each page must necessarily come either before or after any other. But the patterns themselves have no natural sequence. We've ordered them to suit our own tastes, striving only for the most enjoyable reading experience from the first page to the last.

Whether you read them straight through or nonsequentially, bear in mind this cautionary note: We make no claim to the universality of our observed patterns. They certainly don't apply everywhere. A given pattern may fit your organization or not. If it does, we hope it helps transform what before had only been a hunch into an observation you can express, test, and refine with your team.

In writing this book, we have been constantly aware of our debt to the architect and philosopher Christopher Alexander and his admirable book *A Pattern Language*.[2] In this seminal work, Alexander and his coauthors articulated a few hundred patterns about architecture. The book helps us better understand the buildings we occupy—and the ones we'd like to—and it also shows us the way that thoughtfully articulated abstractions can elucidate any subject.

---

[2]See C. Alexander et al., *A Pattern Language: Towns, Buildings, Construction* (New York: Oxford University Press, 1977).

1 Adrenaline Junkies

The organization believes that frenzied activity is a sign of healthy productivity.

The phone rings.

> "We really have to fix a requirements specification this week. Can you come and see what you can do with it?"
>
> "What's wrong with the specification?"
>
> "We were in a hurry, so we got a bunch of new hires to write it. We think they don't know what they're doing."
>
> "Then wouldn't it be more productive for us to coach them in writing requirements?"
>
> "But we need the specification this week."
>
> "Okay, I'll come tomorrow."

Two hours later:

> "Can you come and look at our estimates?"
>
> "What happened to the specification?"

"We don't have time. We'll go ahead with the
requirements as they are. My boss wants the estimates
to be handed in today. . . ."

You probably recognize the characteristics of the adrenaline junkie
organization: Priorities are constantly shifting; everything is needed
"yesterday;" there's never enough project time before delivery; every
project is urgent; and the urgent projects just keep coming. Everybody
is frantically busy . . . all the time.

People in these organizations do not think strategically. Work
gets done on the basis of its urgency alone. Unless a project's "frantic
factor" is high, it will be ignored—even though it promises a significant
long-term advantage. It will remain ignored until it suddenly (surprise,
surprise) becomes urgent. Adrenaline junkies believe that the best way
to work is not by planning but by running as fast as possible.

This kind of culture equates desperate urgency with effective
performance. If you are part of such a culture, it is difficult to avoid
becoming addicted: Urgency is encouraged. The programmers who
work through the night to meet an absurdly short deadline are lionized
(never mind the quality of what they deliver). Teams that routinely
come in on the weekend, just to keep up with their workload, are
regarded more favorably than those that don't. Moreover, if you're
somebody who does not work excessive overtime and are not freneti-
cally busy all the time, then you are not "one of us"; you are not one of
the busy-busy-busy people who keep the organization afloat. Non-
heroic activity is plainly not acceptable.

Most adrenaline junkie organizations contain at least one bot-
tleneck. This is the hero who makes all the design decisions, is the only
source of requirements, or makes all the architectural decisions. He is
playing two roles: One is to make himself appear to be busier than
mere mortals can hope to be. The second is to produce a logjam of
decision-making that once released, causes the rest of the organization
to become even more frantic.

Most adrenaline junkie organizations enthusiastically embrace
the customer service ethic: They confuse responding to urgency with
admirable responsiveness. When a customer makes a request, regardless
of its potential for profit (or even usefulness), it instantly becomes a
project, often with a ridiculously short deadline. (See Pattern 38,
"Project Sluts," for more on this.) This new project naturally increases

the workload on the already overloaded heroes, so more busyness comes about—all of it feeding the insatiable need for the organization to be very, very busy. Many of these organizations think—falsely—that this is what being agile is all about.

Adrenaline junkie organizations react rather than consider. The result is that most things are in a state of flux, and nothing is settled or long-term. The fluid state persists: Specifications are fluid—nobody really knows what to build. Designs and plans are fluid—they will almost certainly be changed tomorrow. There is no attempt to prioritize by importance or value—there is just urgency.

There is no Betty Ford Clinic for adrenaline junkie organizations, and there may well be no cure short of eliminating the adrenaline junkies and replacing them with managers who understand that the organization is most effective when it is not in a state of emergency. Such a replacement may well be impossible, though: It is usually upper management, and often the CEO, who wants to see the organization in a constant state of frenzy. After all, frenzy sustains the illusion of healthy productivity. And if the managers of a company are adrenaline junkies, then project teams are not far behind.

Adrenaline junkie organizations don't always fail. Some of them continue to operate at a frenzied pace for years. But none of them can ever build anything big—that requires stability and planning. Junkie behavior is not scalable—it is limited to what can be achieved by a relatively few people working very, very hard with little direction or strategy.

Naturally, in any organization, there are times when things need to be done urgently, and there are some roles in an organization that need to concentrate on urgent tasks. But all things are not always urgent, and all roles are not concerned with urgent matters. Unless urgency can be replaced with prioritization and restraint, there is little hope of curing the addiction to adrenaline.

2 Rattle Yer Dags

The project team exhibits a palpable sense of urgency to determine who needs to do what by when, and a desire to carry out all necessary actions immediately.

Imagine that you are a fly on the wall during the regular meeting of a development team. You can see and hear the following interactions almost as soon as the meeting gets under way: *What problem are we trying to solve? What are the major elements of a solution? Who is taking the lead on each? What are the first things that need to get done? Who will do them? By when? If we don't know how long a particular task will take, who is scoping it and by when will that be done? When do we need to get back together to plan the next steps?* Done.

After the meeting, often within the hour, an e-mail is circulated, summarizing the agreed plan of action. By the time the summary is distributed, it's not unusual to find that one or more of the action items have already been completed. People had started to work on them, immediately after the meeting.

Even from the wall, your fly eyes can see that this is a high-velocity team.

On one particularly high-velocity team we know, it is not at all uncommon to see people taking action on agreed-upon items *during* the meeting itself. Typically, the person assigned figures it's easier to do the task than to write it down to do later; for example, "Reassign all remaining open priority 2 bugs to Product Management for triage." If a decision can't be made until someone outside the meeting is consulted, the person assigned IMs that person and reports the result to the group, allowing the action plan to proceed.

Such immediate-action examples are the exception, and they are admittedly enabled by technology. But the underlying behavior comes from the team's *culture,* not its equipment. Whether it took the team ten minutes or ninety minutes to reassign the bugs is beside the point; the team *started* right away. You can observe several characteristics of teams that routinely *rattle their dags:*[1]

- *They have an instinctive sense of time urgency.* They see delay as a real risk to success. They don't need to be hectored with deadlines. They strive to get the product to market (or the system into production) as soon as it can be done properly. They understand the money-value of time.
- *They have great confidence in their individual and collective abilities.* Think about walking barefoot through a dark and unfamiliar room. When you are unsure of what is in front of you and you don't know what you might bump into with your next step, you slow down. Your lack of confidence acts like friction. Action-oriented teams are highly confident in the correctness (or correctability) of their decisions and actions, so they feel safe to move quickly.
- *They believe in the value of iteration.* They're not terribly worried about getting it wrong—in part because they are confident, but also because they fully expect to make frequent assessments and course corrections, as they go. Relieved of the burden of making perfect decisions every time, but confident that they will be right most of the time, they decide and act with alacrity.

It's probably worth taking a moment to consider the opposite pattern, characterized by "talk show" team meetings—sometimes entertaining, but devoid of action. These come in several varieties:

---

[1] Ask a New Zealander.

- *The quest for perfect information.* Some corporate cultures place more value on not making mistakes than on getting things done. In other words, it's safer to do nothing than it is to do something and get it wrong. Such cultures breed leaders and teams that seek enough information to make the exactly correct decision the first time. Team meetings often result not in decisions about what to do, but in decisions about what additional information to gather before making a decision about what to do.

- *The cult of "on hold."* Weak teams are far more likely than strong teams to place decisions and action items "on hold." The very concept of being on hold goes against the bias for action that you find on strong software teams. Strong teams yearn to get things done. If a decision needs to be made or a task accomplished, the team is all over it. If a decision is appropriately deferred to a future time, the team schedules it for a specific point in development. Weak teams are always finding reasons to wait until later to make a decision or take an action.

- *The parade of left parentheses.* Poorly led team meetings ricochet from topic to topic as thoughts arise, opening one issue after another, but closing none of them.

- *Tales around the campfire.* Some team meetings are so formless that they consist of nothing more than a series of anecdotes and reminiscences of current and past events in the organization's lore.

- *All roads lead to design.* When the team is dominated by architects and developers, we sometimes observe that every meeting, regardless of purpose or agenda, eventually devolves into a design discussion. Design discussions can be wonderful, but not when they prevent deliberation of other worthy topics.

- *The meeting to schedule additional meetings.* What all failed meetings become.

3 Dead Fish

From Day One, the project has no chance of meeting its goals; most people on the project know this and say nothing.

The goals of many IT projects can be summarized simply: We need this set of functionality, with this accuracy, with reasonable robustness, by this calendar date. The team is assembled, and the statements of goals and constraints are worked into detailed requirements and designs; and they're published.

The big secret is that nobody on the project believes that the project can be an outright success. Usually, the deadline is not attainable with the other goals unchanged. Mysteriously, no one declares that there is a big, stinking, dead fish of failure already smelling up the project.

As the Greek tragedy plays out, the project will slog on. Then, typically a few weeks before expected delivery, each project member, project manager, manager of a project manager, and anybody standing remotely near the project, will either

1. declare shock, dismay, and amazement that the project is nowhere near where it needs to be for the upcoming release

or,

2. lay low and say absolutely nothing about anything unless asked

Why do so many people in so many organizations spray reality deodorant rather than simply state, "No way this project is happening the way we want. The dead fish is here."

Many organizations are so driven for success that anyone expressing doubt gets no reward whatsoever for speaking his heartfelt opinion. In fact, if someone identifies the dead fish in the early stages of a project, upper management's first response is likely to be

> "Prove it. Show us that the probability of success is 0 percent. Draw no conclusions from the other dried-out fish carcasses lying around from previous projects; your project is different. Prove to us with irrefutable mathematics that failure is inevitable."

Anything short of a masterful proof gets lambasted as whining or an attempt to get out of some good-old, honest hard work:

> "Are you a weenie or a layabout? Take your pick, but we doubt you'll be a part of this fine organization for long."

In such an environment, it is safer to "try hard" and not make it than to declare goals unattainable as defined. Granted, sometimes it *is* necessary to take on a very challenging project and give it a real try before conceding anything. Absolutely—but the difference is that on hard projects with real deadlines, nobody waits until the last minute to declare an emergency. If your project is building software for a communications satellite that is set to launch in 18 months—and you know that if you miss the launch date, the next opportunity is 16 months after that—then you and everyone else will be sniffing the air every day for that aquatic scent. One whiff of that aquatic scent and you will spring into action, knowing too well that on a dead-fish project, action waits until most options are lost.

Clearly, the dead fish is not only destructive to organizations, it is demoralizing to the dead-fish project teams and their managers. No matter what the organizational culture, nobody is ever comfortable sitting on a stinking dead fish for long. The costs of keeping a dead fish secret are huge.

> Just for Monty Python fans:
> "This project's not dead; it's pining for the fjords!"
> "It's not dead, it's just molting!"
> "This is a dead project. It has joined the project choir invisible!"
> "And now for some pattern completely different...."

4 Happy Clappy Meetings

Display of high morale becomes a factor in personal performance evaluation.

High morale is an unfailing indicator of organizational health. Similarly, low morale is a sure sign that something is wrong. There is a certain

Chris Linn, Corporate Entertainer (www.chrislinn.com)

kind of managerial mind that seizes upon this relationship and attempts to exploit it in reverse. The logic goes like this: Force morale up and other good things will follow.

Ah, but how to force morale up? In particular, how to do it without investing all the bothersome time and energy and expense necessary to make things truly improve? That's a tough one, but don't think people won't try. Thus the sour humor of the saying, "The beatings will continue until morale improves."

A common attempt to force morale is a ceremonial meeting in which the boss, smiling broadly, stands in front of the assembled group and opens the floor: "Let me hear what you folks have got to say," he tells them confidently. "Anything at all, even the bad news and the hard questions." Note the tone here and the subliminal message: There is nothing to hide because we're all a big, happy family. (Happy, dammit, happy. Pay attention.)

> *At one company I know, the happy clappy ceremony is called an All Hands Meeting,* all hands *because everyone is invited to attend. But when one brave soul actually held his hand up and asked the CEO a hard question, the result was not exactly what he might have hoped. The CEO mumbled something and quickly got off the stage. Later that day, the impudent questioner was called on the carpet by his immediate boss and disabused of the illusion that hard questions were actually welcome. After that, the meetings were unofficially called No Hands Meetings, since it was understood by all that no one was to raise a hand to take part.*

—TDM

When you get the sense that what is being solicited is not your input but only your approval, you know exactly what's happening: Welcome to another happy clappy meeting.

5 Nanny

The project manager has many skills in common with those of the traditional English nanny.

A good manager is aware of the capabilities of his staff. He assigns responsibilities and makes plans to suit the best match between skills available and the nature of the task. This much is obvious. There are some managers who go one step further: They provide a working environment—both technical and sociological—that maximizes people's abilities to use their skills and to improve them. These managers ensure their staff has the tools they need to do the job. These managers encourage questions and debate among the staff; they give each team member the appropriate challenges; they criticize where necessary; they provide a workplace where people enjoy their work; and they make the adjustments necessary to keep things running smoothly. In short, good managers *nurture* their people like nannies nurture their charges.

A *nanny,* in the traditional English sense, is employed by a family to take care of the children. The nanny—usually trained to be a teacher, nurse, and cook—is responsible for the physical, emotional, social, creative, and intellectual development of the children. On a day-to-day basis, the nanny makes sure that the children are safe from harm, and that they get enough fresh air and exercise, eat nourishing food, and learn more about the world and how to live in it. Apart from looking after the children, the nanny also communicates any concerns about their development to the parents, while encouraging the special talents of her charges. The nanny creates an environment where it is safe to take risks and to learn.

When managers have these nanny-like qualities, they get more and better work from their people by fostering and developing their talents.

> *The best manager I ever worked for was Peter Ford. There were obvious things, such as his making sure we all had the facilities we needed to do our work. For instance, we had an open plan office—not the best environment for thinking work—and he managed to get the budget for some sound-absorbing screens and to reserve a couple of "quiet rooms" for our team. All of this, and many other things he did for us, involved negotiation and politics that we were unaware of. He encouraged us to read and discuss new ideas in systems development. He brought books and magazines for our team library and scheduled time for us to discuss them together. He noticed when we were feeling unhappy or unwell, and he talked to us and helped us. He protected us from the rest of the organization, but if he was unhappy with us, he let us know. His office door was rarely closed. Peter was our nanny.*
>
> —SQR

There may be some nannying already going on in your organization if you notice one or more of these conditions: You don't have to make an appointment to see your manager, or you don't have to spend much time on trivial and irritating administrative tasks. The environment has an atmosphere of openness; people say what they think, and they learn from each other. The manager treats training and education as a necessity rather than a luxury, and there is time set aside (like the morning coffee powwow or the Friday afternoon book review) for discussing new ideas together.

In any group of people, there will always be rumors and gossip and the time-wasting activities that accompany them. However, in an office blessed with a nurturing manager, this time-wasting is minimized because the manager makes sure the team knows what is really going on. People don't have to rely on the rumor mill to know what's happening in their organization. Instead, they feel informed and trusted, and they focus on their work.

A nanny-like manager thinks of himself as an enabler of work. While the traditional nanny's job satisfaction comes from seeing the development of the children's abilities, the "nanny" manager gets his satisfaction from seeing individual team members develop in their roles and become more productive and more satisfied with their work.

You see the opposite of this pattern when a manager's attention is on politics, administration, procedures, and kowtowing to more-senior managers. Drawing and adjusting PERT and Gantt charts seem to be more important than talking to the team. And some managers do much of the actual development work instead of looking after the needs of the team.

How does your organization view the role of a manager? Does it reward managers for being work enablers? Does it hire nannies or administrators?

6 Referred Pain

The project solves the apparent problem but fails to address its underlying cause.

Referred pain is a term used to describe the condition whereby pain is manifest in parts of the body other than the location of the source. For example, spinal injuries are felt in places other than the spine. Sciatica is a case in point: The patient feels pain in the leg, yet the problem is a prolapsed disc pressing on a nerve in the spinal canal. You can treat the leg as much as you want, but the pain will persist—its underlying cause lies else-

where. Similarly, a person who suffers a heart attack usually feels referred pain in the left arm. Treating the arm will do nothing to save the patient's life.

There is a tendency when forming projects to address the obvious problem—the one that is most manifest and causing the most pain to the client. However, by looking only to the referred pain, the project delivers a product that, once delivered, turns out to be largely wasted as it does little to alleviate the real need.

Consider the following example: Bank customers who forget their password apply to the security department to have the

password reset. This involves complex and costly processing to authenticate the customer before a new password can be issued. At one U.K. bank, resetting passwords cost in excess of four million pounds per year. A project was formed to build new software that would make resetting passwords easier and cheaper.

This project set out to treat the referred pain instead of the root cause of the problem (too many people forgetting their passwords). Because of a baroque password setup protocol, users ended up with passwords that didn't stick in their minds and the bank experienced "I forgot my password" requests far in excess of what its competitors were receiving. If the bank had addressed the real problem, it could have—at a fraction of the cost—so reduced the number of requests that the existing password-reset approach would have been quite workable.

One commonly observed reason for treating the referred pain and not the cause is a reluctance to investigate. This is sometimes because of the organization's culture, and sometimes because pressure is being brought to bear on the project to start delivering quickly: "Listen, I know exactly what I want, so just generate these reports for me, pronto." In many organizations, it takes a brave analyst to first ask, "If you had these reports in hand, what would you use them for? What are you actually trying to do?"

Sometimes, we want to look where the light is shining brightest. For example, we may look to technologies that we know, seeing the problem in a way that best matches our familiar solutions: Ask a Web services designer how to solve a business problem, and he will typically suggest a Web services solution; ask a database designer, and you'll get a database solution. Needless to say, either could easily disregard any part of the underlying problem that does not slot neatly into his preferred implementation. Moreover, we may be tempted to look to the most attractive problem to solve—the one that will deliver the coolest product. Either of these could result in the engineer rushing to find an ingenious solution to the obvious or stated problem, but exercising his abilities to the wrong end result.

A strong indicator that you are treating referred pain often involves workarounds. These crop up when the current system shows signs of needing some correction, and instead of correcting the prime system, a workaround—allowing something to go wrong and then fixing the result—is applied to correct the manifestation of the problem. A workaround is a Band-Aid and does little or nothing to address the underlying cause of a problem. Yet when one seems to work, more of them are used, sometimes on top of each other in layers of workarounds. Each time a workaround is used, the Band-Aid appears to be cheaper than surgery.

The root causes of many problems are subtle, and often quite removed from the apparent symptom. However, effort spent investigating the real need, and solving the right problem, is invariably returned severalfold.

7 Mañana

We all have windows of time within which we recognize that we need to start moving and keep moving to complete some work. Delivery dates beyond those windows create no sense of urgency, and therefore little motivation to act.

What if Paul Revere took his midnight ride through the villages and towns of Massachusetts shouting, "The British are coming! The British are coming! Sometime next year—I'm not exactly sure when or where, but next year, the British are coming!" [1]

You've got to expect that he just wouldn't have gotten the response he was hoping for. He probably would have been met with angry shouts of "Put a cork in it, Paul!" He may have even met with the occasional projectile chamber pot.

A sense of urgency is a magnificent catalyst for action. Remove that urgency, and that action slides down the list of Things To Do Today. Other matters become more compelling, and today is consumed by all the other stuff that consumes days.

We all have windows of time within which we recognize that we need to take immediate action in order to complete some work. For most of us, the window is about 30 to 90 days out. We can look at ourselves today, and see the path of work ahead for the next 30 to 90 days. We can plan our work for those days, and we can feel the urgency. We get a move on; we get an eagle-eyed focus on what needs to be done.

Outside that window is mañana. Mañana is our state of recognizing personal responsibility to complete some work—without recognizing that we must commence work *now* in order to be successful.

Most projects are longer than the human window of urgency. People cannot feel the urgency in their soul when the organization tells them that it is incredibly important to complete a project within the next 30 months. They hear it; they understand why it is important; but a little voice inside their head says, "Thirty months, by then you could be dead."

Big projects stay out of mañana by keeping most people focused inside the window. They do this by directing the work toward tangible deliverables inside 90 days, often inside 30 days. You hear proposed deliverables like these:

> "Let's build a prototype of the trading screens—just for the bond traders, within the next two weeks."

> "Let's build the code so the system can take in new orders, check if the items are in stock, and send a message to fulfillment. Don't worry about changed or cancelled orders or anything else, just new orders. We should be able to demonstrate this by mid-month, all right?"

The wonderful thing about project people is that they can take on these near-term tasks as though they are up against the actual finish line. On basically healthy projects, people will work hard and stay focused on the prototype due in two weeks, just as if they are delivering the final system in two weeks.

Be careful, though: The key is a real deliverable at the end of the window. Progress alone is insufficient. Something like "Let's get the spec to fifty percent complete by the end of May" just does not supply satisfying closure. The little voice says, "Fifty percent—that means *not done* by the end of May. What other work do I *really* have to complete by then?"

Watch out for a particularly virulent form of mañana: inordinate amounts of time spent getting ready to get started. Everyone spends time hunting for the perfect tools to support testing; everyone debates exactly how the libraries will be set up to provide the best possible support for the developers. This time has much more value if it is saved for finishing the work at the end of the project.

Sheila Brady, recalling her days as a project manager at Apple, had this observation about mañana versus what is in the line of sight:

> *"There has never been a project that, as it came down to the finish, wouldn't die for an extra week on the schedule."*

Like all good project managers should, Sheila realized that the early days of the project are not treated as preciously as those at the end—and that the best way to get going is to get going, not mañana, but today.

---

[1] For those of you not familiar with American history and folklore, Paul Revere is said to have ridden on horseback through villages and towns one night, just before the American Revolution, warning the colonists that the British were coming and preparing them to fight the British at the Battle of Lexington in 1775. There is a poem, *Paul Revere's Ride*, by Henry Wadsworth Longfellow, that every Massachusetts schoolchild memorizes. It ends with this:

> "So through the night rode Paul Revere;
> And so through the night went his cry of alarm
> To every Middlesex village and farm,
> A cry of defiance and not of fear,
> A voice in the darkness, a knock at the door
> And a word that shall echo forevermore!
> For, borne on the night-wind of the Past,
> Through all our history, to the last,
> In the hour of darkness and peril and need,
> The people will waken and listen to hear
> The hurrying hoof-beats of that steed,
> And the midnight message of Paul Revere."

No mañana for Paul; he had a natural sense of urgency.

8 Eye Contact

The organization tends to co-locate project personnel when the work is both urgent and complex.

The trend toward geographic distribution of projects is now well established and probably not going to go away. You know the case for it as well as we do. You may have found yourself making that case to the people who work for you, to explain why most of the staff is right here in town while there are minor outposts in Kissimmee and Richmond-upon-Thames. It's all about money and availability, right?

And yet, 'fess up now, if your *life* depended on the project's outcome, wouldn't you want all the people working on it to be in the same location, able to look each other right in the eye? Of course, there is always the possibility of some available remote person with a specific talent that simply can't be matched by anyone at the site where the rest of the project is located. If that's the case, you might be willing to pay the price of distribution, but otherwise not. The key here is that the justification for fragmenting work ought not to be money and availability; it ought to be about rare talents and skills. And the more urgent the task is, the more co-location becomes necessary.

There is a certain magic that happens when full-time, dedicated project members occupy the same space. They begin to learn each others' needs and capabilities, and as they learn, they modify their own approaches to take best advantage of the mix. This notion of teamwork is closely akin to what we observe in a smoothly functioning hockey team, for example. The nearly invisible signaling that synchronizes the interaction is dependent on physical proximity.

Similarly, on a development team, there are key kinds of signaling that are necessary for close interaction. The most essential of these is the giving and gaining of trust. You can communicate via e-mail and phone with a distant team member and know some things fairly precisely: specifics required by the person on the other end as well as promises made and solicited, for example. If asked, you would say that you believed what the other person had conveyed to you, why not? But if instead you were asked, "How strongly do you believe what you just learned?" the answer would show a marked difference, depending on where the other person was. Promises made and needs expressed by a co-located team member come with body language and history; they are transactions in the midst of an evolving relationship. You know what they mean. The same promises and needs communicated across continents and oceans arrive largely without context.

It's difficult to give and gain trust across a distance. It's also difficult to pick up nuance, confidence, certain kinds of irony and sarcasm, intent, strength of conviction, hopelessness and helplessness, energy level, and deviousness. Without these shades of meaning, the communication limps. The big picture comes through, but the conclusion you draw from it must remain tentative. Can a project proceed with this deficit? Sure, but it is never going to work as well as it would if co-located.

In Pattern 14, "Face Time," we assert that necessarily distributed teams can take important advantage of even occasional opportunities to meet in person. Eye contact takes this to the next level. If the project is important enough, distribution to pick up fungible resources located elsewhere makes no sense at all. Conversely, if it's okay to make use of any available bodies spread out across the country or across the globe, the project is demonstrably not of primary importance. In organizations where eye contact applies, urgency and complexity are trump cards that can be used to secure co-location of the project team.

Where all justification for co-location is ignored (*cannot* be tolerated), the distributed team myth has been swallowed whole by management. Anybody, anywhere, who happens to be coming available when a project begins, is *the* natural candidate to join the new project team. In such an environment, teams are teams in name only.

9 Management By Mood Ring[1]

"Mood Ring" by Bruce MacEvoy

The manager reports status based on the activities, efforts, and enthusiasms of the team rather than on the risks, decisions, and issues facing the project.

Listen to project managers talk about their work. Listen especially to how they communicate the status of their projects. It often reveals quite a bit about how they manage.

Following is a status summary from a manager we'll call Donna. Although this example is extreme, it is representative of many real reports:

---

[1]Mood rings became popular in the U.S. during the 1970s. The idea behind the mood ring was simple: You wore it on your finger, and the color of the stone reflected the state of your emotions. For a few dollars, you could figure out how you were feeling.

"I am delighted to report that we are just about Feature Complete for this release. There are a couple of stragglers, but I am just so proud of how much the team has accomplished and how hard everyone has been working to get to where we are. And judging by the big smiles I see around the office, morale remains high. I am grateful to have such high-performing team members, and I just know they will get the few remaining features finished any day now.

"On a sadder note, I am sorry to have to report that Bob Jensen has decided to leave the company. Bob has been a mainstay of our QA team for over five years now, and he will be missed. Bob's departure follows the retirement of Kathy Enright just last month. As you know, Kathy was also a very experienced tester, so you can bet that our QA manager is starting to sweat bullets.

"I, too, am a little worried about the state of test development for the new features. It's too soon to jump to any conclusions, so just let me say that I'm feeling a little uncomfortable. While I am sad to see great coworkers and good friends like Kathy and Bob ride off into the sunset, our QA team is famous for stepping up in tough times, and I know it'll be burning the midnight oil. We should know more as time goes on."

Notice some things about how Donna described the state of the work:

1. She spoke in terms of the high level of activity, her team's earnest effort, and everyone's enthusiasm for the project.
2. She focused on the *present,* plus or minus a little bit, without reference to the overall framework of time, resources, and deliverables within which her team is operating.
3. When she identified things that were not going according to plan, she spoke of them in terms of the emotions they evoked (for example, "I, too, am a little worried about the state of test development. . . .").
4. Her observations are generally open-ended and continuous (for example, "I just know they will get the few remaining features finished any day now.").
5. Despite the occasional negative note, the overall tone of the report is optimistic.

You may be asking, What's so bad about managers being optimistic and displaying a little emotion? Nothing, of course. But when you find a project manager whose communication is skewed very strongly to this end of the spectrum, you will typically discover two problems. First, this style of reporting does not really fulfill the most fundamental purpose of all project status reporting: It does not focus our attention on the elements of the effort that are in greatest need of immediate corrective action in order to maximize the probability of success. It doesn't tell us what current conditions need our attention, decisions, and action on this project over the next few weeks. Because of the way Donna described things, all we have is a qualitative assessment of a few aspects of the work, with no clear sense of the relative magnitude of any of the issues.

The second condition that frequently accompanies this kind of communication is even more pernicious: Project managers who focus exclusively on open-ended, present-tense activities often do not have a clear sense of the ultimate outcomes they are trying to achieve. They—and their teams—are simply putting one foot in front of the other, as quickly as possible. Yet these teams are most likely to discover only at the last minute that they have no hope of shipping on time, or that they have drifted so far off-course that what they can deliver is not what was promised.

We spoke earlier about Donna's communication style being at one end of a spectrum. Let's hear from Lisa, a manager at the other end of that spectrum:

> "We hit our Feature Complete date last week, on the twenty-eighth of April. Of the eighteen components that make up this release, fifteen of them are now Feature Complete; two more will be complete by the end of this week. The final component, the Data Warehouse Interface, is running even later; we don't expect it to reach Feature Complete until May twentieth. QA is presently assessing what level of re-prioritization would be needed to absorb this slippage, or whether this may cause us to propose moving the ship date. QA will have a recommendation for our next core team meeting on May tenth. In any case, Product Management has agreed that we can do the public beta next month without this feature.
>
> "The automated regression suite for existing features is complete as of this week, and we are now running

it nightly. Pass rates are in the eighty-percent range, which is typical for this time in the release cycle. We expect to see pass rates in the ninety-percent range within four weeks, in time for the delivery of the public beta.

"Development of new feature tests has been slowed by the resignations of two QA engineers over the past thirty days. Recruitment of replacements is under way, but we have to assume that they will not be onboard and effective in time to help us with this release. QA is assessing the possibility of borrowing a couple of people from the support team to help out. We should know how this loss will affect test coverage of the new features within a week, but for now, we have to assume that we will not hit the Test Development Complete milestone on schedule."

Lisa's status summary is different from Donna's in several ways:

1. She bases her assessment on the status of deliverables that are appropriate to the nature of the work now going on.
2. She focuses on outages, issues, and proposed changes to plan, and she identifies the required corrective actions and decisions.
3. Her observations are discrete, not continuous, and most are measurable.
4. She offers a balance of objective and judgmental information.

Very few managers communicate exactly like Donna or Lisa. Most of us are somewhere in between. Nevertheless, it is worth watching out for the Donnas. A pattern of consistently focusing on effort over progress sometimes reveals a manager who does not comprehend the difference between steering and navigating.

Oh, and by the way, it's especially important to look for Donna in the mirror. If you find your own communication veering that way, ask yourself whether you might be doing so because, like Donna, you are not all that sure where your team should be going, just that everyone is working really hard to get there.

10 True Believer

An individual embraces a school of thought as gospel. Even slight deviations from the canon are considered sacrilege.

Nearly all of the popular methods in software engineering arose from practitioners' experience, not from basic research. People were motivated to write down what worked for them on their projects, and the experience got transferred from a small group to many others. By communicating with many of the leading process designers, we know that most of them concede that (1) their methods were developed for certain domains or project sizes and (2) their methods have never been expected to work exactly as described for all possible environments.

> *Our CASE tool ProMod, in its early versions, flagged as errors a lot of things that our customers considered okay. Whatever methods we implemented, we did them by the book—we were true believers. Whenever the text suggested something or showed an example, we abstracted from that and coded it into hard rules. We flagged it as an error when a user did not exactly follow our rules. Only over time did we learn to flag things as warnings instead of errors. Even more, we learned that we had to make all of the messages optional; in*

other words, we let the user decide whether to turn them on or
off, and we allowed the rules to be violated.
                                                                        —PH

Although most process books contain fair warnings about the applica-
bility of the methods, true believers either ignore these warnings or
never make it to the pages that contain them, which are usually found
toward the end. Currently, it is very much the vogue to be an XP
advocate, even among people who have never read the penultimate
chapter of Kent Beck's first book, in which he clearly explains the limits
of the approach.

> *One of my clients is considered by her boss to be a major*
> *success factor because of her software engineering skills and*
> *enthusiasm. We discussed UML activity diagrams in their*
> *latest variety, Version 2.1. I was surprised to hear that she*
> *refused to use the UML tool chosen by the company "since it*
> *did not support all the new features such as n-dimensional*
> *swim lanes, interruptible regions, and parameter sets." Instead,*
> *she preferred to use Visio shapes, which gave her the freedom to*
> *follow all the suggestions of the new action language. She*
> *claimed she really needed them all. She was a true believer.*
>   —PH

True believers on your project can bog the work down. Instead of con-
centrating on the content, they fight methods wars. Often, true
believers are found among consultants brought on board to help with
methods. The ultimate clash is achieved when two principals (either
insiders or consultants) turn out to be true believers of two different
methodologies. Bring on the proxy wars! No matter how good they
are, you'd be better off without either of them so you can get on with
your business.

> "Different methodologies are needed on different
> projects."
> —Alistair Cockburn, *Agile Software Development*
> (Reading, Mass.: Addison-Wesley, 2002), p. 162.

11 Lease Your Soul

The practitioner is willing to abandon a long-mastered skill or technology.

An admirable characteristic of the competent professional is a willingness to shape solutions to the problem to be solved, rather than force the problem to match the tried and tested competencies of the individual or team. That does not mean that team members lack skill in applying the tools and approaches they know. *But instead of selling their souls to any technology, they lease them.* In other words, when good new ideas come along, they are ready to consider their merits, compare them with past technologies, and make intelligent decisions about using the most appropriate approach.

In Goethe's story, Faust makes a pact to sell his soul to the devil.

It is not always easy to abandon a long-held—and mastered—technology, but soul leasers are able to live with the temporary discomfort involved. They know that their current technology is sufficient, but they also know that a newer technology may offer something more. While they are not sycophants to every flavor-of-the-month technology, they are prepared to set aside their familiarity with their current way of working and consider the merits of any genuine advance. Their attitude is that of looking to the future, not of seeking reassurance from the present.

The advantage of being a soul leaser is that one is not left stranded when the tide of technology turns. You probably know people who refer to themselves as developers but have not attempted to learn a new programming language in many years. You know these people:

They are the ones scouring the job offers for a mention of their language, which is one in the long litany of once-contemporary, but now almost unused, programming languages. Sadly, these developers sold their souls to that language.

For organizations, it is not so easy to be a soul leaser, but there are advantages that outweigh the difficulties. Naturally, any organization cannot arbitrarily change its technology. It needs a certain amount of stability in its languages, development methods, technological infrastructure, and so on. We are talking about an attitude here. When an organization decides that it will investigate new technologies continuously, it sets out its stall to attract the best and brightest potential employees. It is saying, "Here is an organization that is moving with the times. Work for us and we won't leave you stranded in a technological backwater."

Newness does not always equate with goodness. When a new technology—a programming language, modeling technique, methodology, software tool—is released, it is usually accompanied by persuasive publicity and, in many cases, a large helping of hype. Sometimes, the new technology is seen as a *silver bullet,* something that will make a huge advance in the state of the art. In some cases, people fall under the spell of the hype and become mindless enthusiasts, in the process selling their souls; as a result, they see every problem in terms of the new technology's solution. Soul leasers, by contrast, separate the promises from the practicalities, and because they clearly see where the advantages lie, they can pick and choose from the benefits of new technology.

Technology moves on at a breathtaking pace, and today's sparkling innovation is often destined to become yesterday's rusting hulk. Soul leasers, both organizational and individual, possess a light touch with their technologies. While enthusiastically embracing a new technology, they know this is only a summer romance, and they make no greater commitment to it than using it, faithfully and skillfully, until the next advance overtakes it. The question they ask is, "What problem is this suitable for?" and not "How do I solve this problem using this technology?"

Being able to separate the problem from the solution is the first step to becoming a soul leaser. The second step is to know that no matter how good the technology is, there will be something better tomorrow. Try not to make the Faustian pact by selling your soul to any technology.

12 System Development Lemming Cycle

Although the organization's process calls explicitly for tailoring, the project team still slavishly adheres to the un-tailored standard.

Driven by CMMI, SPICE, ISO9000, or other process improvement programs, many companies set up in-house standards for their development processes. Naturally, these process models come with prescribed roles that members of the development team must fill, the activities they must perform, and the artifacts they must create. Most of the process models acknowledge that not all projects are created equal. Therefore, some of them (such as the German V-Model and the Rational Unified Process) come with extensive tailoring guidelines to adjust roles, activities, and results to project constraints.

Tailoring the process and (especially) pruning the results requires courage. If you leave out certain steps or decline to create some of the required deliverables, you leave yourself open to criticism if the project fails. Critics will be quick to point out that the project would have succeeded had you been more faithful to the process and created all the suggested documents. The fear of criticism—or perhaps the fear of punishment—can bring about a reluctance to tailor. The result is that the team plays safe, produces a full-blown requirements specification with all the suggested chapters and paragraphs, creates the quality management plan (including sections for each milestone), creates work assignments for each package in the work breakdown structure, and so on, for the full extent of the process.

> *When I asked Philippe Kruchten what he would change, he replied to the effect that if he could develop the Rational Unified Process one more time, he would make tailoring and adapting the process to a specific project much easier and tool-supported to encourage projects to really do it.* —PH

Lack of courage is not the only reason for not tailoring. Often, the reason is much simpler. Tailoring a process to fit the project's constraints requires work. And the project manager is simply too busy with other, more-urgent project matters to brainstorm and establish the rules for the game. The argument goes something like this: *The company has hired clever people (outside the project team) to define the processes and the deliverables. Why should we question their wisdom? Let's simply go for it. They can't be that wrong. And—by the way—nobody pays me for changing the process to fit my constraints. So let us not waste time on process adaptation; we'll simply do it the way everybody does it. That way, we can start with project stuff immediately.*

Sticking to a process that is poorly matched to the project's real needs can get the work started earlier, but not finished earlier.

A project manager not tailoring the process is like a cook working strictly from established recipes. He will never become a great chef. Of course, even great chefs start out as apprentices, learning the basic mechanics of food preparation from their masters and copying their masters' recipes. But they will only stand out if they learn more than the basics of the trade and stop cooking from standard recipes.

13 No Bench

The organization has become so lean that the loss of a key person proves catastrophic.

If you've ever set a second alarm clock or stashed some extra money in your glove compartment, "just in case," you know you were practicing the most sensible kind of risk management. Things go wrong, and the way you protect yourself is to have some duplication of resource.

If you run a project team made up of professional knowledge workers, losing a key person is likely to be your most conspicuous risk. So of course you have an understudy or two tucked away, haven't you? Maybe just one or two people with a range of skills that would allow them to step in easily for any one of the project principals? No? Really? How can this be?

The reason you don't have reserves is that they cost *money*. (Pay attention here, this is important.) If reserves were free, you'd have a bunch of them, but they aren't, so you don't. The dictates of efficiency require that you utilize as few people as possible to do the work that needs to be done. A starvation economy may not be much fun, but it does make efficient use of resources, doesn't it?

The problem with this reasoning is that it is all about money and not at all about time. On most development projects, time is a scarcer resource than money. Your project, at some point in the future, may find itself short on time, and when that happens, you and the management above you will wish you had the opportunity to spread around a little cash in order to buy some time. But that late in the project, opportunities to buy time are few.

Having some staff "on the bench" is potentially a way to trade money for time when a key person leaves. If you apply these reserves thoughtfully, you may be able to partially duplicate some of the key project skills. You will by definition extend your team size beyond minimum cost, but your reserves won't be idle. They will be somewhat overqualified for the work assigned to them while on reserve, since they possess the skills required to step in as understudies, if needed. The advantage is that when you do lose someone, an acceptable replacement may already be on-site and ready to move rapidly into the role. Your project will lose less time this way than if you only begin to search for a replacement after you lose a team member.

14 Face Time

The distributed project team relies on lots of face-to-face contact among the sites, to build the familiarity and credibility that enables long-distance teamwork.

> "At computer society meetings one continually hears young programming managers assert that they favor a small, sharp team of first-class people, rather than a project with hundreds of programmers, and those by implication mediocre. So do we all."

Some of you will recognize this excerpt; others may be surprised to learn that it was first published more than thirty years ago.[1] You still hear this today, though "programmers" have become "developers," and today's managers also specify a preference for a small, *co-located* team of rock stars. It was true thirty, forty, and fifty years ago, and it remains true today—this is the best way to build software.

And yet, large and geographically distributed development teams seem to be more common than ever. You may encounter project teams spread across half a dozen or more development sites, though two or three sites form the more common configuration. Granted, a large

---

[1]Frederick P. Brooks, Jr., *The Mythical Man-Month: Essays on Software Engineering* (Reading, Mass.: Addison-Wesley, 1975), p. 30.

distributed team may be composed of smaller co-located teams, but it must be managed as a distributed team if the sub-teams are working on elements of an integrated system or product.

Regardless of the motivation, distributed development may be proliferating simply because the availability of collaboration technology makes it less daunting. Teams cope with the challenges of distributed development by using instant messaging, wikis, video-conferencing, and Web-based meetings, in addition to good-old conference calls and e-mail.

Those who make distributed teams work best are careful to introduce opportunities for members of the group to get together at least occasionally. Why is face-to-face contact so essential to the success of distributed teams? In the absence of adequate face-to-face contact, teams at one site tend to regard those at the other sites with disdain. "Other sites" often comes to mean "bozos." Face-to-face contact that is regular, reasonably frequent, and cross-functional builds up the reserves of goodwill and benefit-of-the-doubt that we spend down on all those conference calls and Web meetings.

So, how much face-to-face contact is enough? This varies from team to team, but these general guidelines may help you to decide for your project:

- Those most responsible for coordinating work among the sites need the most frequent contact. These people usually carry titles like program manager, project manager, or release manager. They need to meet multiple times per release cycle. Meeting quarterly is not enough.
- Among developers, QA engineers, and technical writers, the more-senior people need to meet their counterparts at other sites at least once per release cycle. Establishing mutual credibility and respect at this level enables opinion leaders to influence more-junior team members back home.
- Occasionally allowing junior team members to travel to other sites helps them see how their work fits into the team's overall mission, and it exposes them to mentorship and career development with senior people at other sites. It also helps when you are arguing for a raise for your wunderkind to have a peer at another site support your high opinion of him.

Consider the following fool-proof recipe for guaranteeing the failure of a distributed development effort: Following the acquisition of a team at a distant site, the organization responds to the inevitable pressure to cut costs by restricting business travel "temporarily, until things improve." To succeed at distributed development, you almost certainly will have to increase, not decrease, your travel budget.

Distributed development is an inherently difficult, high-risk practice. Sometimes, the potential to access or retain desirable talent justifies the risk. To borrow Tom Wolfe's phrase, "I don't *advise* it, you understand, but it *can* be done."[2] Face time is one essential element.

[2]Tom Wolfe, *The Right Stuff* (New York: Farrar, Straus & Giroux, 1979).

15 I Gave You a Chisel. Why Aren't You Michelangelo?

The manager buys tools in the subconscious hope they can bestow skills upon the team.

Software tools are often sold by bright-eyed young men who make extravagant promises about the tool's effect on productivity and the powers it will bring to those who use it. It is safe to say that most consumers see through the exaggerations of advertisers' promises—effortless weight loss; learn a new language while you sleep—but the ability to separate reality from illusion sometimes deserts harassed IT managers.

These managers are under pressure to produce, and they have too few resources to do so. An automated tool is sometimes seen as a lifeline, and in a giddy moment of desperation, the tool buyer overlooks the notion that the tool's user must have the appropriate skills.

"The cost of a tool is more than the cost of the tool."
—Dorothy Graham

What we are looking at here is a matter of appearances. The presence of tools on the desktop conveys a sense of the developer's competence and productivity. Yet, the tool by itself does not change anything: Productivity does not automatically increase, the reported error rates stay depressingly high, and morale, discouragingly low. And while the facts say otherwise, the belief persists (somehow) that productivity bottlenecks can be broken open by wielding a checkbook.

Why aren't you Michelangelo? can be heard in organizations desperate for an immediate productivity gain, and where recruits are hired less for their skills than for the paucity of their salary. Michelangelo organizations almost always have an extensive library of shelfware.

Of course tools are useful, and in the right hands, they bring on wonderful productivity gains and allow things to be done that otherwise could not be done. But as the builder of a tool will tell you, having the right skill to use it is crucial. A chisel is just a piece of metal with a sharp edge until Michelangelo picks it up.

16 Dashboards

Release	Aug 9	Aug 2	Jul 26	Jul 19	Jul 12	Jun 21
Chelsea	Aug 31	Aug 31	Aug 31	Aug 31	Aug 15	Aug 15
Kennington	Oct 20	Oct 20	Oct 20	Oct 20	Oct 20	Oct 20
Kennington Server	Nov 15	Nov 15	Nov 15	Nov 15	Nov 15	Nov 15
Hounslow	Dec 22	Dec 22	TBD	TBD	TBD	TBD
Hounslow for Linux	Feb 14	Feb 14	TBD	TBD	TBD	TBD
Hounslow for Solaris	TBD	TBD	TBD	TBD	TBD	TBD

Dashboards are used by strong teams and weak teams, but typically not by average teams.

Google the term "dashboards" and few of the results will have anything to do with automobiles. Over the past decade, dashboards have become a very popular way to visualize and communicate the status of a project or business process.

A dashboard is a document or Web page that displays a collection of metrics—usually both graphically and numerically—to provide an overall picture of how well the project or process is performing. Some dashboards allow the user to "drill down" to see more-detailed information about performance elements summarized at the top level.

Like many dashboards, the example above uses a color scheme to indicate the relative health of various aspects of the project or business process. This is one of the most popular schemes; it employs the three colors commonly found on traffic lights: green, yellow, and red.

With color schemes and simple design, dashboards can be quite effective and beneficial. However, they can also be a complete waste of time. The difference has little to do with the dashboard and everything to do with the culture of the organization that is using it.

The best teams use dashboards to focus their collective attention on making the most important decisions and taking the most important actions, all at the right time. The underlying belief is that (1) at all times, certain conditions are reducing your project's probability of success; (2) these conditions are sometimes difficult to detect; and (3) you can improve your chances of success if you take corrective action on the most important issues, soon enough. Good dashboards help you focus on the conditions that need correction.

Weak teams use dashboards to affix blame on others or to deflect blame (by conveying good news).[1] To tell whether you are on such a team, look for these signs:

- *Red means failure.* If this is the team's belief—explicitly or implicitly—then your team uses its dashboard as a pillory. A dashboard should be used to share status indicators, such as colors, to highlight what needs to be adjusted for the project to succeed. If people conclude that red casts them in a bad light, they are far more likely to hide *exactly* the conditions that most need to be exposed. Avoiding the use of red for fear of blame is like disconnecting a smoke detector because it makes too much noise.
- *Orange is red in denial.* Weak teams can't handle the truth. They want to see everything optimistically, and they want to avoid raising alarms. Their dashboards reflect this outlook. Orange is just red seen through rose-colored glasses.
- *Green means don't look too closely.* Often, teams stay green longer than they should—until the status is switched to red, at the last minute. On some teams, anyone who declares that an aspect of the project is yellow or red will be challenged to prove that the item is not green. The implication is that yellow or red means "you're screwing up." The inevitable effect of such a culture is that all items will remain green until failure is imminent; then red is assigned, when no options for corrective action remain.

These practices are superficial symptoms of a deep and usually fatal problem: Teams that operate like this are driven by a fear of criticism, not by a passion for success. Teams inherit such traits from their leaders. Dashboards don't improve leadership, they reveal it.

---

[1]See Pattern 45, "News Improvement."

So, what are some of the traits of effective dashboards? Here are a few:

1. *Dashboards don't overwhelm us with data.* The surest way to defeat any project control scheme is to report everything. Great dashboards report a carefully chosen and very limited set of metrics.

2. *Dashboards are editorially selective.* A team's dashboard is in some ways the team's weekly newspaper. The process of deciding which information is on the front page—and which is buried three levels deep—sharpens the team's focus.

3. *Dashboards are more judgmental than informational.* Some dashboards look like a corporation's annual report. You'll see page after page of tables and graphs, all very factual and objective but mostly useless. These dashboards provide lots of information about what's going on without addressing the real question: Is this okay or not? Effective dashboards provide information, but they also convey judgment.

4. *Dashboards are predictive as well as reflective.*[2] Some teams use their dashboards as scoreboards, to report on what has happened. Effective dashboards also attempt to predict what will or will not happen in the future. For an example of a kind of dashboard that is designed to be predictive, see *The Balanced Scorecard: Translating Strategy into Action.*[3]

5. *Dashboards show trends over time.* A surprising number of dashboards present nothing more than a snapshot of the project or process. However, unless the work has come to a complete and final halt, this is not a sufficient set of telemetry. Teams also need to understand the trajectory of the effort. If an item is yellow, what color was it before? Is it getting better because our corrective actions are working or getting worse, trending toward red?

6. *Dashboards provide a framework for making comparisons when teams must report a subjective assessment.* Dashboard assess-

[2]See Pattern 49, "Journalists."
[3]Robert S. Kaplan and David P. Norton, *The Balanced Scorecard: Translating Strategy into Action* (Boston: Harvard Business School Press, 1996).

ments are not absolutely objective; they do—and should—reflect the judgments of the team members. When they do, it is important to state what the judgments mean. You might be surprised at the wide variety of incompatible definitions we've heard for designations like red, yellow, and green. Just for the record, we prefer these:

- Green: The effort is on-track and likely to meet expectations, without major course corrections.
- Yellow: Substantial and/or immediate corrective action is required in order to meet committed dates and other expectations.
- Red: The effort is now off-plan. It either has missed a date or will soon, unless drastic action is taken, probably involving at least some replanning.

We've used the green-yellow-red model here, but these definitions apply to many kinds of status report. Regardless of their style or format, effective dashboards share this single most important trait: They focus the team's attention on what needs to be fixed *immediately,* to improve the probability of success.

17 Endless Huddle

The right of infinite appeal ensures that no decision is ever final.

Many project teams do not regard any decision as final. Apparent acceptance of a decision merely indicates a determination to pick up the fight later on. Decisions made during January come back for re-discussion and re-decision in February, March, and beyond.

The worst effect of this behavior is squandering time, the project's most precious resource. Project leadership has many decisions to make during the course of the development cycle. Making one decision over and over again almost guarantees that it consumes more time than it deserves and that the most important decisions receive less attention than they require. Moreover, if Marek, Zelda, and Zac are spending their time grumbling about the decisions they disagree with, they are not using their energy to move the project forward.

Why does this happen? The endless huddle can be so pervasive that it appears to arise from the culture of the organization. But the root cause of the endless huddle is the team's leader. Team members who disagree with a decision will appeal it just as long as the leader tolerates it. It is up to the leader to know when to break the huddle and to have the courage to do it.

A characteristic of an established profession is an effective decision-making process that contains the rules for making decisions along with rules for what happens afterward. *Warfighting*, the United States Marine Corps's concise publication about military doctrine,[1] contains a well-understood set of decision-making rules:

> "Until a commander has reached and stated a decision, subordinates should consider it his duty to provide his honest, professional opinion—even though these may be in disagreement with his senior's. However, once the decision has been reached, the junior then must support it as if it were his own."

But there must be some disagreement with decisions. How do marines avoid the endless huddle? They accept that once a decision has been made, they must abide by it. They recognize that there is a difference between abiding by a decision and agreeing with it. There is little point in telling people that they must agree. If you have a different opinion, then the fact that someone has made a ruling is not going to change your opinion. Abiding by a decision means that you will take the defined action and not spend energy fighting against it—regardless of whether or not you agree.

Avoidance of the endless huddle requires a decision-making process that suits your project. For example, the product design company IDEO realized that it needed a defined way to choose between designs without dampening creativity.[2] During the first part of each project, groups within the project team investigate the problem and create some kind of prototype. Then each group presents its prototype to the rest of the team, giving everyone a chance to state his opinion and recommendations. After the discussion, each project team member casts a vote for his preferred design idea. If there is no consensus, the project manager decides which path to follow. This procedure works for IDEO because everyone knows what the process is and what tangible artifacts will serve as input to the decision-making process. So, all team members abide by the decision once it has been made, regardless of whether or not they agree. And the project moves forward.

---

[1] *Warfighting*, United States Marine Corps (Washington, D.C.: 1997), p. 59.
[2] Tom Kelley, *The Art of Innovation: Lessons in Creativity from IDEO, America's Leading Design Firm* (New York: Doubleday, 2001).

Endless huddles happen when people believe it is acceptable to abide by a decision *only* when they agree with it. It is the manager's job to establish an ethic of abiding by decisions and living with them once they have been made.

18 Young Pups and Old Dogs

The organization with plenty of young people (in their twenties) is more vibrant than one filled with old farts.

You can be forgiven for reading the first part of the pattern and thinking, "We have reasonable numbers of young people in our organization." But then you hit the parenthetical expression, and thought, "Uh, oh . . . not *that* young."

When you find an organization with a critical mass of youngsters, the place is almost bound to be hardworking, upbeat, relaxed, and, in the best meaning of the word, *fun*. Everyone seems to be happy to be at work. Young people bring a sense of excitement with them. They haven't been working full-time for very long, they are learning skills, and they are learning that they can become competent at difficult work. They are enthusiastic, they want to work, and best of all, they want to do a good job.

This keeps all of us Old Dogs on our paws and not snoozing in the corner. We have to run with the youngsters, and we become "younger" doing it. Though they are rarely represented at the top, young people are the rhythm section of the entire organization. They set the pace. Most importantly, they set the pace for learning. They're young; they're learning. That's what they're supposed to do.

For us Old Dogs, much of our knowledge comes from ten or more years ago and is now irrelevant. To stay at top-value, Old Dogs need the learning pace of Young Pups.

Contrast this with Very Old Dog organizations. Very Old Dogs are just about completely populated with folks in their forties, fifties, and on up. They have become this way from one of three causes:

- *The organization is not growing, and there is little opportunity to hire youngsters.* This happens frequently in places like government agencies where those who built large systems a decade—or several decades—ago are now maintaining them. For some people, it is a comfortable life, with good retirement and health benefits at the end of the trail. Managers in these organizations usually say it is hard to find a youngster willing to work there.
- *The organization has decided to hire only experienced people.* If this policy stays in place long enough, there are no Pups at all. "Fifteen years of XML experience required, an intimate understanding of JCL a plus."[1] Who would have these qualifications? Not a hot gun just out of a university.
- *The organization is downright unadventurous.* It does not intend to deploy any new technologies that only young people know about. Nor will it embark on risky ventures that would require new and different talent. And in this kind of organization, the established managers do not want to be challenged by Young Pups who know things the Old Dogs don't.

The obvious way of stopping your organization from becoming an Old Dog (or a Very Old Dog) is to hire youngsters. But not everybody can do that. You must have positions available, and you must be willing to

---

[1] JCL is intentionally inserted for the amusement of Ancient Dogs.

invest in your newcomers. However, it is easy enough to consider getting some college co-ops to work part-time. There are also summer internships.

Dare we even mention high school students working after school?

19 Film Critics

Film critics are team members or corporate spectators who have determined that the value they add to the project lies in pointing out what has gone wrong or is going wrong, but who take no personal accountability to ensure that things go right.

You are in the final weeks before releasing your new system into production. Integration testing has been in full swing for some time, and the developers are fixing bugs as they come in. Release managers are going though their checklists of pre-ship activities to ensure that nothing has been overlooked. Then, at a readiness review, a new voice is heard. This is typically someone who has been associated with the project since its inception, but who has had little to say until now. We'll call him Herb.

Herb is not all that pleased with the state of things. Herb feels that the product about to be shipped has missed a few key features. And the design reviews were not all they could have been. And the integration testing should have been far more rigorous. Given all of the problems he sees, Herb feels that shipping the system now may pose serious risks. He has enumerated the risks in an impressive PowerPoint deck that he has e-mailed to the world.

You consider Herb's points, and you have to agree that some of them are valid. But your overall reaction is, "Why are you telling us this now? Where were you when we had time to address these issues?" Herb waves off your questions, offering no constructive suggestions for correcting what he sees as deficiencies, but reiterating his concerns about the way things have been handled.

Herb is a film critic.

Sometimes, on projects, film critics have real jobs and their criticism is more or less a hobby. Other times, they are actually chartered to be film critics by a manager who values this behavior. Either way, all film critics share one trait: *They believe that they can be successful even if the project they're on is a failure.* They have, in effect, silently seceded from the project team.

Not all project critics are film critics. A lot of the difference is in the timing. People who feel accountable for the success of the project tend to speak up right away when they see that something is going wrong or could be done better. They come forward and say what they think, to whomever they believe can make a difference. They do so as soon as they can, because they know that time is always short and that corrective actions should be taken sooner rather than later. These people are not film critics; they are your fellow filmmakers. They know that they cannot succeed if the project fails, so they are taking matters into their own hands, every day, to increase the probability of your collective success. You may agree or disagree with their criticism, but you can see that they are working on the same film you are.

Pursuing the analogy between projects and films, we note that film critics don't tend to weigh in until the film is complete, or so near to completion that there isn't enough time left to take corrective action. It's not that they actually want the project to fail; it's more that they have come to believe that their own success is independent of the project's success and has more to do with being seen as a keen observer of the obvious and an accurate predictor of the inevitable. They don't necessarily realize it consciously, but they no longer care whether the project succeeds or not, as long as they are seen as having been right.

Why are some projects infested with film critics while others have few or none? There is only one reason: Some management cultures emphasize doing things right, while others emphasize not doing anything wrong. When managers are most concerned about not making mistakes, or at least not being seen as having made mistakes, they send obvious signals, both explicit and tacit, that catching people making mistakes is just as valuable to the organization as doing things right. Those people in the organization who have natural film-critic tendencies rise to these signals and engage in freelance film criticism on their current project to see how it will be received. If it is tolerated, or even rewarded, then film critics will multiply and accountability will diminish. Keep in mind that it is far easier to be a film critic than it is to be a filmmaker, that is, to be an accountable leader or team member. If the organization demonstrates that it values film critics, it shall have them.

Film criticism can exist at all levels in an organization, and it even can be institutionalized in a number of ways. The most common case is the unofficial film critic. This person already has a role on the project, though typically a peripheral one. Many film critics are in staff support roles, and from there, they can criticize multiple projects. In an especially diseased management culture, senior leaders may even charter an entire organization to act as a watchdog on teams building systems.

On project teams, film criticism is one example of a more general destructive pattern that we call goal detachment. Notice what enabled the film critic: the belief that there were multiple ways to succeed on this project. The project itself could succeed, of course. But the film critic (or the leader who chartered the critic) allowed that goal to be replaced by a related but independent goal: to accurately identify what's going wrong on the project. It's not that identifying deficiencies is a bad thing; it obviously is not. Goal detachment is destructive because people pursuing detached goals are only coincidentally working toward the success of the project; their efforts are just as likely to be inconsequential or even counterproductive.

20 One Throat to Choke

There is a clear mapping between each project task and a single responsible individual. Each person knows precisely which responsibilities are his own and which belong to his colleagues.

In a well-run restaurant, the responsibilities for work are clearly divided among the team members. The saucier makes sauces; the pâtissier is responsible for the pastries; the maître d' tends to greeting and seating; the sommelier focuses on the wine; and the scullery maid washes the dishes. If you observe the work patterns, you see how each person focuses on the tasks for which he is responsible. The waiter pins an order onto the orders clipboard and takes a basket of bread to the table. The head chef scans the order and shouts the dishes' names to each specialist. The fish chef cooks the halibut; the saucier makes the sauce; the vegetable chef prepares the watercress garnish; and the presentation chef puts the dish together. When the dishes are ready, the waiter is summoned and carries them to the table. Each individual knows what he has to do, when he has to do it, and just as importantly, what to expect of his colleagues. The atmosphere is alive, busy, and purposeful. When you find this pattern in a project, you can feel the same buzz of excitement and achievement in the air.

What is actually going on here is that people thrive on having responsibility and knowing exactly what that responsibility is. The business analysts know what is expected of them; the testers know what their connections are to the deliverables; the business users know precisely what is expected of them; the developers know where their tasks start and stop; the project manager knows his responsibilities for steering and allocating tasks . . . every individual on the team is confident of what he has to do and how he will know when he has done it.

In accepting the singular responsibility for any piece of work (a component, assignment, objective, or action item), the individual knows and accepts his responsibility because that work is clearly mapped to an expected outcome. The individual thinks, "It's up to me; everyone is counting on me for this—I am responsible for *my* work." Similarly, each person on the team knows the responsibilities of others and thinks, "I can count on specific colleagues for these things."

An organization that has this pattern can also cope when unforeseen things happen and nobody is responsible for dealing with them. People are used to having responsibility and consequently are not afraid to take charge of a task that needs an owner.

Having sole responsibility does not preclude asking for help and getting critical input from colleagues and any other relevant sources. The point is that the designated individual is still responsible for the agreed component. That person knows and agrees that "for this component, it is my head on the block. . . ."

This is very different from giving someone a job title and assuming that everyone will interpret the responsibilities of that title in the same way. What happens in these cases is that nobody really knows precisely what is expected of anyone. The consequence is uncertainty, fear, erosion of confidence, waste of human effort, and a great deal of pfaffing around.

Some projects operate on the basis that everything is everybody's responsibility. The thinking, on the surface, may seem admirable: "We are a team. We pull together, and if anything needs doing, then it is everyone's responsibility to make sure that it gets done." Not surprisingly, this approach rarely works. Imagine such a team running a restaurant. In between cooking soufflés, the chef would be worrying about making reservations; the waiter would add some extra salt to the soup; the maître d' would wash the odd dish, to ensure there were enough for table 22—everyone would be worrying about (or interfering with) everything and not doing anything particularly well.

The power of having one throat to choke comes from the confidence that people get from understanding what is expected of them. And this provides a clue for how to encourage this pattern in your own projects. You need to be able to characterize a component so that there is an objective indicator of what it is and how everyone will know if it has been delivered. The component may be the delivery of a specific module of software, the responsibility of providing feedback to the developers on the quality of their design, or the development of user training for a new product. The issue is that the component can be characterized so that everyone has the same understanding of what it is. If you can do this, then you can allocate singular responsibility to an individual and have everyone reap the benefits of improved work facilitation and personal confidence.

Interlude:
Project-Speak

Harmless sounding words and phrases disguise ominous ideas.

WHEN THEY SAY:	THEY REALLY MEAN:
The schedule is aggressive.	We're toast.
We will make up the slippage in the next few iterations.	We're still toast.
He's the point man.	He's toast.
executive summary	cartoon version
high-level	not for real
rapid staff buildup	NFW
Manager of Special Projects	manages his own desk
We're from Corporate, and we're here to help.	(no translation needed)
Work continues.	We're clueless.
Time will tell.	We're clueless, and we admit it.

This has been a learning experience.	We really screwed that up.
Having said that . . .	Everything that I said before was BS.
code complete	not tested
You are empowered.	You're taking the blame for this.
low-hanging fruit	Something even [insert name] can't screw up.
Let's put this behind us and move on.	(means the same thing it means when a politician says it)
Now, take my advice.	I outrank you.
The code has become unmaintainable.	I would have designed it differently.
We are still at 30,000 feet.	It is on my desk, untouched.
Bradley here is our wild card.	Bradley here is the Project Idiot.
Get on the same page.	Do it my way.
best practice	invented by people who don't work here and therefore infinitely superior to anything we do
Leverage core competencies.	Don't do the hard stuff.
Take it off-line.	Make it go away.
You have a novel approach.	You are an imbecile.
Testing has turned out to be a major bottleneck.	They keep finding bugs.
limited release	function-free release
Let me clarify what I need.	New requirements incoming!
We are considering our options.	all one of them

21 Soviet Style

©2007, Milan Ilnyckyj, sindark.com

The delivered product has the functionality requested by its customers, and yet it is disliked and soon discarded.

More and more of us book our travel using Web sites. When you use a travel site, you enter origin and destination, date, number of passengers, and so on, then select a flight from the search results. If you want to rerun the search to check whether flying business class makes a difference, some sites make you reenter all the data you just entered. If you are patient, you may find a flight that pleases you, but chances are, you'll grow annoyed enough to give up and try some other provider. Companies with such inferior usability usually go out of business quickly. But that does not stop other companies from making the same mistakes.

You have probably used some of these Soviet-style products that do more or less what they are intended to do but in a way that you find awkward or irritating. You find that the products' usability is not what it should be; their look and feel is unattractive; they lack certain security aspects you feel are needed; or they contain cultural references you find disconcerting or offensive. These are failures to meet the products' nonfunctional requirements—those that make them appealing to the humans who use them. Such requirements are every bit as important for eventual acceptance as the functional requirements.

Consider the iPod. It represents the opposite of Soviet style. At the time of this writing, the iPod is the most popular portable music player in the world, commanding about 80 percent of the market. Why is it so popular? It wasn't the first MP3 player on the market, nor the cheapest. It does what any other MP3 player does. Its success is largely due to its nonfunctional qualities—its attractive packaging, ease of use, capacity, battery life, small size, and—let's face it—its sheer coolness. These are the nonfunctional requirements that are often overlooked by project teams.

The reason that nonfunctional requirements are often neglected is in part historical. For many years, systems analysis methods concentrated on functional requirements, expressed in notations that captured the functions and data of the products. These methods assumed that somebody else would deal with the requirements for quality of service. The methods were more than a little vague on exactly how an analyst might capture nonfunctional requirements. Analysts knew perfectly well how to specify a use case and draw entity models or activity diagrams, but none of those are any use when addressing nonfunctional requirements such as cultural suitability or look and feel.

> *When I was about thirty-five, Tom DeMarco gave me my first pair of scissors made for left-handed people. It was a revelation; I could actually use the scissors with my left hand, and I could actually see where I was cutting.* —TRL

It is not difficult to tease out the system's nonfunctional requirements. Templates are readily available to guide you through all of the important quality-of-service categories. Successful teams make systematic elicitation of nonfunctional requirements a special path in their process, constructing usability models and employing specialists in these areas.

Customer complaints will tell you if you have built a Soviet-style product. Another indicator is an unusual amount of rework and modification. Alternatively, you may receive a lack of feedback—say, fewer than expected bug-fix and enhancement requests—this may mean your customers are not using the product at all. In all of these cases, of course, it's too late—you've already spent your development money.

How can you avoid building a Soviet-style product? Make sure your project plan includes tasks explicitly focused on nonfunctional requirements. That sounds easy, but consider that most Soviet-style systems got that way because nonfunctional qualities were simply ignored. Beyond an ongoing focus, use early project prototyping to generate meaningful feedback on the nonfunctional qualities that will win user affection.

22 Natural Authority

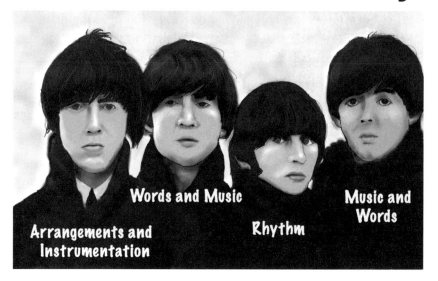

Words and Music

Music and Words

Arrangements and
Instrumentation

Rhythm

Competence attracts authority.

Authority tends to move toward and congregate around competence. In a multifunctional team (and what other kind is there these days?), different team members have differing degrees of competence in different domains. The authority to make decisions wants to follow that competence.

Knowledge work is profoundly different from production. In a production environment, workers share a common and usually simply stated goal ("Put out the maximum tonnage of Rice Krispies in the next eight hours"), and also share the skills necessary to get the work done. The boss is typically someone who is master of these skills, and also the one who has the deepest understanding of the line and how it functions. When decisions need to be made, the boss is the one to make them.

In knowledge work, on the other hand, the skills are diverse, as is the understanding of different aspects of the problem. A given decision lies in the natural domain of one or more team members, and these are the ones who should make it. If the decision touches on others outside the team, the natural-domain team members need at least to be party to whatever decision is eventually made.

In common English usage, there are several meanings given to the word "authority." In one meaning, the person who knows a great deal about a given subject is considered *an authority;* whereas the person who is in charge of an effort is said to be *in authority.* It is quite possible to be an authority without being in authority. Similarly, one could be in authority without being an authority. The healthy pattern is that each decision is made by people who *are* authorities, whether or not they're *in* authority. (It is still possible, even likely, that the person who takes responsibility for seeing that a decision is implemented may be someone in authority rather than the decision-maker.)

The opposite of this pattern is obvious: Decision-making follows lines of hierarchy instead of knowledge and mastery. Those higher on the control hierarchy make most of the decisions, sometimes without consulting those with a better understanding. This is what happens, for example, when national political leaders make key decisions about the tactics of warfare. It is also what happens when technological decisions are made in the organization as a function of price, with the more costly decisions made higher in the hierarchy, often well above the centers of competence.

Violating the flow of natural authority sounds like an abuse of position, like it's all the manager's fault. But sometimes, a subject-matter expert shares the blame. In this more insidious variation, managers (particularly those who are not so well-liked) are simply given enough rope to hang themselves. People with vital and necessary knowledge sulkily allow a bad decision to be made above them, offering no input beyond what is specifically requested. This is an abandonment of responsibility, since silence gives consent. The silent experts are as much responsible for a bad decision as the knowledgeless managers. But when the pathology is deep and established, nobody much cares.

23 The Too-Quiet Office

The office is too quiet, a sign that the team has lost its mojo.

You can get a pretty good read on a software development team just by walking the halls. Some sites exude energy. Team members move through them with purpose and obvious pleasure. At the other end of the spectrum are sites that seem like warehouses for forgotten software teams. They have no energy at all. People are waiting until they can go home, and they are waiting for that next paycheck to cash, while looking for something exciting to do, or for retirement day to come.

24 The White Line

The project uses the equivalent of the white line on a tennis court to achieve a non-arguable definition of scope.

When you watch a tennis match, you see the clean white lines marking the edge of the playing area. Any ball bouncing on or inside the line is in. All others are out. Most sports involving a ball have a white line and an official to judge whether the action is inside or outside the playing area. Apart from the occasional raised eyebrow at a line call that goes against them, the players respect the white line. The call is clear—the ball has crossed the white line, or it hasn't.

Yet many projects have no white line—they attempt to distinguish between what is inside or outside the system with either a list of features or a statement of goals. Each is too vague to constitute a usable white line.

Any feature in a feature list has to be implemented somewhere, but not necessarily entirely within the system being scoped—it may pass off some or all of its responsibility to an allied system. So, the statement that a feature is included doesn't really define scope, just as it is by no means clear from screen sketches which system is to produce the data shown on a screen.

Similarly, goals are achieved by a combination of actions performed inside the system and immediately outside. (It could be a goal of a new system to speed up receivables processing, but that goal would still depend on the responsiveness of the guy who first enters the receivable data into the system.) It's always worth stating goals for a project, but such statements do not give a clear indication as to what happens inside and what is outside the new system boundary.

So, what can we do to achieve a precise definition of scope? Let us start by considering the nature of what we are about to study: A system or a business area is made up of processes that transform data. This is universal; it applies to any kind of system. These processes alter the state of the data by changing one set of attributes to another before handing it off to the next process. This assemblage of processes and their data is shown in Figure 24.1.

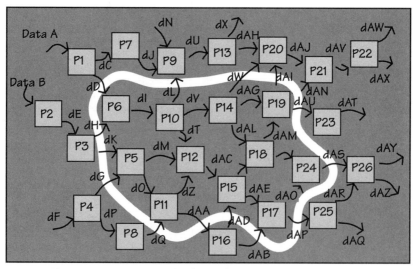

Figure 24.1. Processes both inside and outside the system transform data before passing it along to the next process. Each flow of data is uniquely named to represent its unique set of attributes. By cutting through these flows, the white line makes a clear separation between functionality contained by the system and functionality that is carried out by the outside world.

The data, as it is passed between processes, is unique. At no other point can there be another flow in the same state with the same attributes. Immediately outside the system is another process. The important point is that the interface between the system and the outside is simply another flow of data moving between processes. Like all other flows, it is unique.

By declaring—preferably modeling—each of the unique collections of data items that cross the boundary, you are saying, "The functionality to produce this data is contained on one side of the boundary, and the consuming functionality is on the other." To put it another way, you are defining the scope of your project by declaring each interface between the system or business area to be modified and the world immediately outside. Once you have done that, there is no ambiguity about the scope: You have painted the white line through the interfaces.

25 Silence Gives Consent

A stakeholder fails to distinguish between resigned silence and agreement.

There is a system of commitments that ties together any project. Developers commit to do work on a schedule and to an agreed-upon level of quality; the organization commits to pay salary and benefits and to provide the wherewithal necessary to get the tasks done (infrastructure, support, hardware, access, and so on).

Some of these commitments are very explicit, while others are more or less implied. For example, did your company actually *commit* to provide you with access to all the busy people whose input you'll need in order to finish on time? Or was that only implied?

The system of commitments breaks down when the maker and receiver have different interpretations of whether a commitment has been made and/or what exactly it was. Discontent, when it occurs in an organization, is very often centered on implied commitments that were understood in different ways. Implied commitments can be a trick of the light, taking on a different form depending on where you sit. You may hear a manager complain, "He promised me this deliverable by the first of the year, slipped the date, gave me another date, slipped it, gave me a third date, and now that one is slipping as well." The developer might view the same interaction completely differently: "I never gave him a date; I certainly never agreed to *that* date."

A common way that commitment misunderstandings happen is this: One party expresses need, and the other nods in understanding. The first party takes this as a commitment: "I told him I had to have it by December thirty-first, that it was absolutely essential." The other party takes this as whistling in the dark: "Sure, he'd like it by the end of the year, but that wasn't going to happen." The one who expresses the need is almost always someone with more clout, and he bases his expectations on an old maxim from the legal system: *Silence gives consent.* If you don't say no to such a person, you have said yes.

Silence-gives-consent commitments are bad for everyone. The two parties inevitably attach differing priorities to the work, and it's all bound to end in tears. In the abstract, the problem looks tractable: People have to learn to say no. But the real world is not abstract; it's full of messy particulars. The messy particular we most commonly see is that a project is already overcommitted, new needs appear at an astonishing rate, and implied commitments multiply like rabbits. In such a situation, if you were the overcommitted developer and a manager came to you expressing the need for yet something else to be done by December 31, who could blame you for just shrugging?

A discipline that makes implied commitments markedly more manageable is to declare publicly a small number of important commitments. They are written down and shared with all parties. The maker and receiver of the commitment have to agree on the wording before the commitment is revealed to anyone else. This only works if the number of explicit commitments is kept small and if they are indeed the ones that matter.

There's no commitments book, just a short commitments list. It names the individuals who have promised certain results by certain dates. The committer, in this case, is bound to give priority to public commitments over the other wishes that land on his desk. The rule of silence gives consent is thus repealed: Only consent gives consent.

26 Straw Man

Team members feel comfortable offering a straw-man solution in order to elicit early feedback and insight.

A straw man is not an abstract model. It is a solution. It may be an incomplete and/or incorrect solution, but you intentionally offer it up to solicit client criticism. Your purpose goes back to the world's oldest systems joke:

> *Clients don't know what they want until they see it . . . and that's not it.*

Any really funny joke has a grain of truth in it, and this one is no exception. Clients simply do not know what they want because they have no idea what they can get. The best analysts do not try to analyze their way to a solution. They analyze for some insight, make a minimal commitment to a solution or part of a solution, and quickly offer it up for reaction.

Straw–man models are a form of *requirements bait,* to borrow a phrase from Steve McMenamin. You present clients with idea triggers to draw out their likes and dislikes. The models are quickly done, and they're cheap *because they're wrong*. The client reviews a mock-up, prototype, or storyboard of the solution—say, of the "Homes for Sale in the Selected Area" screen. It's a simulation of what the world will see in the future; in exchange, the client leads you to the real requirements.

The best analysts try to avoid asking, "What do you want?" They recognize that this is often an uncomfortable question. People hate to create an answer from a blank piece of paper, but they do not mind critiquing what is already on paper. Consider this test:

Which task would you be happier taking on?

1. writing a report for your executives, on the pros and cons of building a new data center
2. reviewing a report on the pros and cons of building a new data center, before the report is sent up to the executives

Most of the world is much more comfortable with number 2. Humans are effective improvers, naturally, and few of us are naturally comfortable creating from whole cloth.

> *At the start of a new project, I was at a meeting in which an executive said, "I don't answer questions." This struck me as odd at the time, but in context, he was really saying, "Don't spring on me any open-ended questions that I haven't had a chance to think through. Don't put me on the spot." He was absolutely right. He preferred to have a straw man to point at, to help him decide yes or no.* —TRL

The very best straw-man models may even contain *intentional* errors. Analysts mar the models to keep the client alert and to signal that unfettered criticism of the model is completely acceptable. This takes a tough-skinned analyst, one who can accept "playing the fool" as an advanced practice, to accelerate convergence on a solution. It is the highest form of the straw-man art.

Straw-man modeling is useful whenever people iterate their way to a solution. In addition to straw-man requirements analysis, consider straw-man software design. Offering the design team the first design that comes into your head has three possible outcomes. All are winners:

- After some review, the strategy behind this particular design is outright rejected, and another straw-man design, based on a different design strategy, rises to replace the first.
- During inspection, designers make incremental improvements to the design and eventually agree on a preferred design.
- A miracle occurs, and the straw man is found to be the chosen design. (We have never seen this happen, but it could happen someday, somewhere—just don't count on it.)

The philosophy of the straw man is that by being wrong early and wrong often, you'll get to right as soon as you can. The problems we all face and the solutions we derive are too complex to spring fully formed from the mind of any one person. Get tough and ask, "How's this for an idea?"—even when you know you are flat-out wrong.

Many of you may think that you use straw-man strategy already, but have you ever had someone point at your mock-up and laugh out loud? That is straw man.

27 Counterfeit Urgency

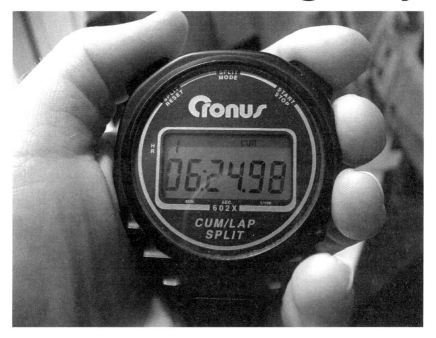

A tight deadline is imposed solely to contain costs.

It's bad to be risk averse, right? If the new century has taught us any-thing, it's that attractive opportunity exists only in risky waters. This premise is so widely accepted today that many organizations have become averse to being risk averse. But somehow that hasn't made everything better.

When organizations aren't willing to take on real risk, they can still talk a good game. Mostly, they do this by asserting the riskiness of certain endeavors that might more precisely be described as mean-ingless. We've all seen our share of these fiascos: death march projects that throw resources at an impossible schedule goal. On the surface, death marches look like gonzo undertakings, initiated by can-do, aggressive risk-takers. Often evident under the surface is a very dif-ferent situation: a project that would simply cost too much if it were completed in the time that prudent estimation would allocate. Gonzo management sets out to do in one year what every sensible participant has said ought to take two. Of course the project is declared to be"extremely urgent," a "unique management opportunity."

To identify counterfeit urgency, we need to look closely at what benefit the project might deliver. If the benefit is real and substantial, then the one-year schedule certainly implies aggressive risk-taking, maybe too aggressive. If there are such important benefits to be gained, why not allocate the time to do the job right?

The far more frequent case is that the benefits are marginal, and that is the reason the effort was underfunded. The apparently aggressive schedule was actually just a funds-limiting mechanism.

Counterfeit urgency produces counterfeit risk. The projects end in tears, but that's not the worst of it. The worst is that the organization hasn't gotten on with the real business of doing high-benefit projects, the ones whose risks are worth taking.

28 Time Removes Cards from Your Hand

Time is a poor project manager.

It's the decisions a manager makes early in the life cycle that have the most impact on a project. For example, a manager's staffing decisions usually need to be made early—not at the outset, but early. With eight months to go on a ten-month project, adding another developer and a tester may well increase the chances of a full-function, on-time delivery. On the other hand, adding that developer and tester with two months to go may not help your odds at all. Indeed, it could lower them a bit. Somewhere between month 2 and month 8 of the project, Time removed the value of adding additional people.

Time can also make shortsighted decisions about what will be in the next release. This situation may be familiar: The next release of the system has already been announced to customers for full function-ality by the end of November. The team is not very confident that it can build, test, and integrate everything for release by that date. The manager isn't too sure either, and he lets everyone know about the team's concerns. The word comes back, "Come on. It's only May. Give it your best shot. That's all we ask."

As the months go by, the picture gets no cheerier, yet nothing has changed in the release plan. Somewhere in mid-October, a Corporate Rocket Scientist announces, "They're not going to have everything done for November." The team gives a sarcastic cheer at this "news." Then the Rocket Scientist proceeds: "No need to panic; we're all adult men and women here. Let's convene first thing tomorrow morning in the Donner Party Conference Room to see what we can do to save face by delivering *something* for the promised November date."

The next morning, the Rocket Scientist starts the meeting by writing on the white board, "November 30—Core Release." He turns to the assembled, and asks, "What shall be in the Core?"

At this point, you are trying not to burst into laughter, because this is clearly a roomful of adults pretending to have a situation in control when Time has taken all degrees of freedom away from the project.

The answer to "What shall be in the Core?" is simple: "Whatever we've got now, dude—it's October already!" Somehow, you now have the equation, "Finished = Core." Anything already done is Core; it's vital to the release. We can prove this to you.

The following is a dialogue you will *never* hear in any Save-the-Release-Date meeting:

Manager: "What shall be in the Core Release?"

Developer: "Well, Matilda has finished this little froufrou component that changes the color of the background based on a randomization routine. It's coded. It's tested. It's ready to go."

Manager: "No, that's not Core."

By the fact that it is done, it must be included in the release. You have to laugh here, or you'll cry. Time has managed this project into a complete bind. By waiting until it was clear to everyone that full functionality was not going to happen for November, Time has steered the project badly in two ways:

First, the project will deliver less than it could have. If the human manager and the team had decided back in May to scrap the Full-Functionality-for-November plan, they could have prioritized the feature set, building and completing features, working down the priority list as time permitted. They would have delivered more features 100 percent done, and some not even started. Time's strategy, on the other hand, produced a lot of features that were close to done. But "Close to Done ≠ Done." What a waste.

Second, Time delivered a misshapen core. Instead of the most valuable features making the cut for the November release, Matilda's distinctly noncritical code and other bits like it get delivered.

All good project managers know when they need to play their cards so that Time cannot trump them.

29 Lewis & Clark

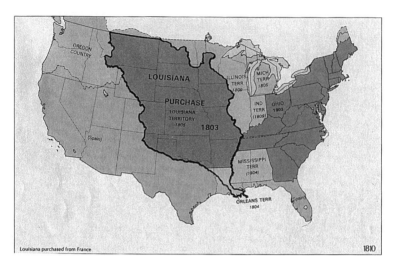

OREGON COUNTRY

LOUISIANA

ILLINOIS TERR *1806*

MICH TERR *1805*

PURCHASE

LOUISIANA TERRITORY *1805* **1803**

IND TERR *(1809)*

OHIO *1803*

(Spain)

MISSISSIPPI TERR *(1804)*

ORLEANS TERR *1804*

Spain

Louisiana purchased from France

1810

The project team makes an early investment to explore the domain and investigate its potential.

In 1803, the United States was made up of the few states that lay between the Great Lakes and the Atlantic seaboard. President Thomas Jefferson extended the country by buying territory from France—the Louisiana Purchase. The Purchase was known only by the description "the drainage of the Missouri River." Nobody quite knew what that meant, including Jefferson. At the time, this was unknown country, inhabited only by the native nations and the occasional French trapper. To find out what he had bought on behalf of the United States, Jefferson commissioned Captains Meriwether Lewis and William Clark to lead an expedition to explore the newly acquired territory and to assess its potential for trade and settlement. A party of 33 people—the Corps of Discovery—set out from Illinois in May 1804. When the explorers returned in September 1806, they brought back maps they had drawn along their route, and information about the territory they explored. These discoveries are well documented in the Lewis and Clark diaries, versions of which are available today in most bookstores.[1]   Now Jef-

---

[1] For the story of Lewis and Clark's expedition, see Stephen Ambrose, *Undaunted Courage* (New York: Simon and Schuster, 1996).

ferson had the data he needed to decide how to take advantage of the territory, and this led to the westward expansion of the United States.

Some projects are a bit like the Lewis and Clark expedition: They allocate budget for exploring the problem space in order to decide what might be possible and whether launching a project into this space is in fact viable.

Such an exploration is, like the historic 1804 expedition, a pure voyage of discovery. You cannot mandate what must be discovered, just as Jefferson could not instruct Lewis and Clark as to what they were to find. And whether the voyage of discovery finds anything useful is not just a matter of chance—the skill of the explorers has an effect on the outcome. Again, like Lewis and Clark, you may find that if the voyage turns up something useful, it may be very, very useful. (Your view of the last sentence may be somewhat different if you belong to one of the native nations that were displaced by the westward expansion.)

The explorers on the project team explore work in the abstract sense. They are not concerned with who is doing what, or what machines or people are used. Instead, they are examining a situation to see what ideas it provokes, what opportunities they can come up with, what the possible future state of that work could be. They are looking for opportunities and ideas that, if realized, will bring the greatest potential advantage to the host organization.

> One of my clients was receiving project requests from more than one hundred different sources. Each of the requests was in a different form and level of detail, but none gave a coherent picture of what the requestor was trying to achieve. The problem was that all these potential projects contained unknown territory and needed some exploration before my client could decide on the appropriate action. And yet, the requestors were always pressing for a firm estimate of cost and a completion date.
>
> My client decided to address the problem by introducing a short exploration of each project request. He used a checklist of exploration questions to analyze the request and to decide whether it contained the necessary answers, or whether further exploration would be necessary before he could quantify the request. Sometimes, the exploration discovered that the cost and benefits of the project did not justify going ahead.

*My client has now changed his procedures such that
a short exploration that answers questions on a checklist is the
only way that a requested project makes it onto the project list.*
—SQR

Lewis and Clark projects deliberately allocate resources to an up-front exploration of the business area to determine the potential for the project. Naturally enough, there are times when the exploration reveals that there is nothing useful that can be done to improve a situation. This discovery is a bonus—it prevents unnecessary projects from chewing up valuable resources. Other times, the exploration team finds that there is indeed an opportunity to be had and launches a project. Such opportunities have a payoff sufficient to cover the occasional barren exploration.

30 Short Pencil

Successive waves of cost reduction begin to interfere with the organization's ability to get work done.

Sure, cost containment is important, even essential. It's vital that your organization has as little burden of overhead as those it competes with. Given all that, there is still something terribly wrong when you start to hear team members make comments like this:

> "I hate working for a company that makes you turn in a short pencil before you can get a long one."

The most dedicated cost-reduction advocate would probably admit that such programs can be carried too far. It's perfectly obvious that too much cost reduction could make an organization less able to compete, and eventually even begin to drive costs up. It's perfectly obvious, but let's take a moment anyway to examine a list of the ways that cost reduction beyond a certain level can hurt you:

- Firing people and allocating their work among their remaining peers may eventually cause those peers to leave and thus necessitate the hiring of expensive new people, all at the bottom of their learning curves, to do the work.
- Overloaded people may begin to burn out, take sick time, introduce defects into the work, and breed discontent.
- High-priced professional workers may spend increasing amounts of their time doing the clerical tasks that had previously been done for them by lower-paid workers (those now trimmed in the interests of efficiency).
- First-level workers may be relatively directionless because the managers who used to look out for them are gone.

- People whose peers have been fired may be just annoyed enough to desert the organization that fired their colleagues. (And they won't time their departures to facilitate the needs of the organization they're leaving.)
- Loyalty, energy, innovation, morale, and dedication may decline while absenteeism, schedule slip, and shoddy work increase.

As you look over this catalog of horrors, consider that each and every effect is accompanied by no-kidding, real cost savings. The company that begins to experience all or most of these gone-too-far symptoms is probably having a terrific quarter, due directly to the attendant cost savings. Income hasn't been much affected yet, and every dollar of revenue is offset by a smaller amount of cost—so net profits look great. But the organization is eating its seed corn.

A single cost-reduction program may very well be sensible. But if your company is now entering its second or even third cost-reduction wave, it may be time to stop thinking about what you can do to help the company cut more costs and start thinking instead about your own well-being. As the long-term effects take hold and revenue declines, a clamor will arise for even more cost reduction, to protect profits. You may be able to hold onto your job in spite of the company's declining fortunes, but it's certainly not going to be much fun.

> *"We need to distinguish between cost reduction and organizational bulimia."*
>
> —Ken Orr

31 Rhythm

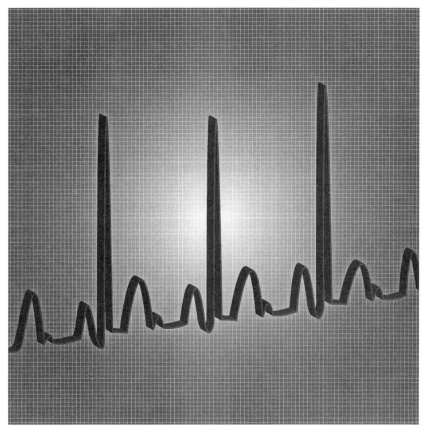

The team establishes a rhythm for its work by delivering at regular intervals.

> *On the third day of a hike from Chamonix to Zermatt, I looked up at a steep, endless, impossible, snow-covered slope. My guide was undaunted—his advice: "Each step brings you closer to the top. Don't look at the summit; instead, concentrate on taking regular steps. Just establish a steady rhythm and maintain it—then you will arrive."*   —SQR

Instead of being daunted by large and complex tasks, projects with rhythm take small, regular steps, thus establishing a regular beat that carries them toward their goals. These enlightened teams work something like this: First, they look up at the summit of the mountain and set the project goals. Then, as a team, they plan what they will deliver within a foreseeable period of time—usually one month. Every day during that month, team members get together and share progress, ideas, and questions, and make plans for the next day. The project goals, monthly target deliverables, and daily feedback meetings set a rhythm for working.

The length of the cycle is not important, as long as people still recognize it as a rhythm. So, one day works well (say, for daily builds) or one week or one month (as in the SCRUM method). Periods of six months or more are outside most people's window of urgency (see Pattern 7, "Mañana"); it's more difficult to respond to such a slow drumbeat. The period must be recognizable.

Projects with rhythm deliver useful products more often and more quickly than projects without it. With rhythm, people get used to delivering something useful at an agreed frequency. Even if one of the intermediate deliverables is less than perfect, the project's rhythm alone can keep the team energized and enthusiastic. Perfection is not expected; delivery is. Not delivering is unthinkable.

The approach works because each individual is fulfilling a bargain with the rest of the team. Working to the rhythm is a self-reinforcing activity—team members produce because of the demand of the rhythm, and at the same time, they find it progressively easier to keep pace with the rhythm. The peer pressure to maintain the rhythm becomes a healthy driving force.

As a manager, you should overcome the temptation to dictate the rhythm or try to increase productivity by upping the tempo. The team establishes its own rhythm that becomes the driver for regular delivery. Even difficult or routine work is easier to do if you do it to a consistent beat. Think of climbing the mountain and establish your rhythm by taking regular steps.

32 The Overtime Predictor

The manager looks upon early overtime as a sign of glowing project health.

A story from our colleague Jerry Weinberg: Jerry was coaching one of his clients, a first-time project manager, and drew him out along the following lines:

> JW: "What can you tell me about Lester, your integration team lead? What do you observe about him?"

Mgr: "I observe that Lester must be pretty confident that we'll make our scheduled date."

JW: "You *observe* that?"

Mgr: "Well, what I observe is that he's working really hard and putting in a lot of overtime. From that, I conclude that he must believe in the date; otherwise, he wouldn't bother."

JW: "Can you think of any reason why he might be working extra hard if he specifically did not believe in the schedule?"

Mgr: "Huh?"

JW: "How might it benefit him to work a lot of overtime if he believes the project is going to miss its deadline?"

Mgr: "Um, I guess he might be thinking that when we miss the date, nobody could blame him if he'd been seen by everyone to put in all those extra hours."

JW: "Uh huh."

Mgr: "...?"

Managers, particularly young managers, are gratified to see people under them putting in extra hours. They take it as a sign that their powers of inspiration and motivation are working well, that everyone is as determined as they are to bring the project home successfully. But there may be a darker possibility at work here: Early and persistent overtime is a likely sign of a project team in fear.

When a culture of fear takes hold of an organization, a host of possible causes may be in play. Here is a list of the usual suspects:

- *Fear-based management:* Some organizations are run by fear, from top to bottom. If you are in one of these, there is no fixing it. Leave; life is too short.

- *Fear of cost-cutting reductions in force:* If your company has been laying off employees to cut costs, or such cuts are rumored, your people may be putting in extra time in the hope that it will help them dodge the ax.

- *Fear of personal failure:* Team members that do not feel confident in their ability to do their jobs sometimes work extra hours rather than ask for the additional training or coaching that might do them more good.

- *Fear of project failure:* If your team members are not sure that the planned schedule allows enough time for them to succeed, they may start right out sprinting. This is a bad thing because it is unlikely that they will be able to sustain a sprint for the duration, which means they will flag when you most need their reserves.

- *Certainty of project failure, and fear of personal blame:* If your team members know that the schedule is a total joke and that the project is doomed from the start, some of them may make a point of working long and visible hours, to ensure that they do not take the blame for the inevitable fiasco.

Not all projects with people working beyond the normal workday are headed for trouble. It is especially common, and not necessarily troubling, to observe a rise in hours worked during the final push to meet release criteria and get the product ship-ready. But when you see significant overtime logged at the outset of the project, you'd be unwise to treat it as a sign of health.

While overtime always presents itself as driven by enthusiasm and professionalism, the real driver is more likely to be fear. Early and persistent overtime is a predictor of less-than-desirable project outcomes, including burnout, employee defections, schedule slippage, and quality compromises that undermine product integrity.

33 Poker Night

"Card Players," by Pro Hart

Employees from throughout the organization get together for activities that are not tied to their work roles.

Right now, the U.S. is going through a poker craze. Groups of seven or eight people will get together at one player's home, once a month or so, to play poker. The beer is cold, the felt table is brought out, the chips are stacked, and the cards are shuffled. Pot Limit Texas Hold 'Em is most often the game of choice. Usually, the players are coworkers, and often a regular will invite a guest player to join the table.

So, around the table might be you (the host and recently promoted product manager), two project managers, the VP of Operations and her friend who does something in HR, a lead developer, and a guy from Engineering whom the developer brought along. There is also a consultant from California who is doing something with one of the project managers.

The game is Hold 'Em, and the only sure winner tonight is the organization. Whenever people get together and break rank and responsibility, the organization gets a little healthier.

There is nothing particularly magical about poker: The vehicle can be any group activity, either social, charitable, or community-based. It can be the company-wide chess tournament or the co-ed softball league. It can be a group of company volunteers brought together for a charitable event, such as a Habitat for Humanity house-construction project or a blood drive. It can be volunteers to man the corporate-sponsored water station for the hometown marathon. The point is that it is a group situation in which the corporate role of any individual is irrelevant to the activity. A marathon runner does not care whether it's an executive or a mailroom clerk who hands him the water cup. Both are equally capable of water cup handling.

The activity is a chance for people to meet each other as men and women, not as roles. The activity is supportive; it is fun or satisfying. The activity is almost failure-proof; although you might lose a few bucks in the poker game, you're not going to feel your time has been wasted. There are chances here for plenty of easy conversation. There are chances here to learn a bit about the other folks.

During the evening, you, the host, find out that the woman from HR is named Molly. She is married to a fellow who is the head technician at a local radio station, and she has twins who are eleven years old. Molly's husband is baby-sitting because Molly loves poker. She has loved it ever since she learned to play as an undergraduate at Purdue. Molly doesn't like beer, and she brought a really nice bottle of Shiraz to the game, to share with any other non-beer-drinkers.

From now on, when you see Molly in the parking lot, you both give a wave. Every once in a while you chat, and she is still trying to talk her husband into twins-sitting again so she can play and win back the $20 she lost last time.

There comes a time when you are desperately trying to hire a great candidate to work in your group, but HR is asking you to go through all sorts of tedious procedures before you can actually offer the position. You are really worried the candidate might slip away. You decide to give Molly a call, and you explain the situation. Molly tells you she'll see what's happening. She calls back and tells you she has lined up a call for you with her boss. You speak with the boss, and the offer goes out that afternoon.

Familiarity offers the chance of trust and the chance of patience. It's easy to be impatient with another employee. It is very hard for Molly to be impatient with you, and it is easy for you to extend some trust to Molly when you need to.

Organizational lines exist for control and decision-making. They don't usually exist to accelerate work throughput. The lines of organizations don't usually adhere to the workflows of the organization. Building personal relationships between people only distantly related on the org chart is lubrication for the important work of the organization.

Many organizations try to lubricate communication lines artificially with assorted team-building exercises. While these may work sometimes, they are usually not nearly as effective, since the individual has no sense of being a volunteer. You signed up to help with the blood drive, and so did the others at the first meeting; that is very different from being told that you are scheduled for an off-site on Wednesday and Thursday to help build corporate identity and spirit. Almost all corporate attempts to enhance trust are lame.

There is no need to force-feed a poker night. Just create situations for people to meet, to have fun, and to succeed together. Whatever you do, no matter how these situations spring up, no matter what you think of the people and the activity, do absolutely nothing to squelch them.

"We are never more fully alive, more completely ourselves, or more deeply engrossed in anything than when we are playing."
—Charles E. Schaefer, ed., *Play Therapy with Adults* (Hoboken, N.J.: John Wiley & Sons, 2002).

34 False Quality Gates

The project's quality assurance activities focus on format checks that do nothing to improve real quality.

Upon reaching a milestone or finishing an iteration, many organizations execute an institutionalized quality check of the results. Very often, this quality check is split into two parts: a check on the existence and form of planned artifacts and a check of the content. The first step is intended to make sure that the expected deliverables have been produced in the expected format. The second step confirms that the content of each deliverable is relevant, accurate, and complete enough for the purposes of the project. The first is syntactic and the second is semantic.

But there is no point in worrying about the syntax of a deliverable if the semantics are lacking.

The languages of our everyday communication—French, English, Albanian, Urdu, and so on—all have their own grammatical syntax. We use this syntax to help us discover and communicate meaning. For example, English grammatical rules say that all sentences must contain a verb. "We eat breakfast in the evening" is a sentence that would pass the syntactical test—but does it make sense? We can only answer that question by doing a semantic analysis to determine whether this is the intended meaning within the context.

Similarly, all the languages of system development have their own syntax. Common examples are a UML use-case model that must have (1) an actor to trigger it and (2) a use-case name; design models that must have a definition of each one of the interfaces; data field dictionary entries that must include ranges of values. However, these syntactic checks do not help if the wrong actor is defined as triggering the use case, the definition of the design interface contains the wrong details, or the range of values for the data field is incorrect. Semantic checking of the use case asks whether the trigger really is the correct, essential trigger for that use case and if there could be other triggers for the same process.

Just because a document passes its syntactic completeness check does not mean that it is fit for a purpose. A data field defined in the dictionary does not mean that its content has been understood. A process description in the style of "get input, do some work, produce output" is just a waste of paper.

> We reviewed a functional specification document that had a heading "Glossary of Terms" in the table of contents. The document was intended to specify functional requirements so that potential suppliers could bid on the job. When we looked at the body of the document, we found that the glossary contained ten entries at varying degrees of vagueness—and these entries did not match the terms used in other parts of the document. But this document had satisfied the quality check because it contained a section called "Glossary of Terms."
>
> —SQR

Organizations that have false quality gates focus on the syntax and form of a deliverable but neglect the content. There are three common reasons for this behavior:

- Persons assigned to do the QA job are not part of the project team and have no interest whatsoever in closely reading and commenting on the deliverable. So, they take the easy way out and comment on the form. On an international project, one of the partners commented on a specification that had been sent out to all partners, in order to freeze the requirements for the next big version, adding this insight: "This hundred-page text document still contains an enormous number of double spaces and thus looks totally unreadable to me. Correct this and resubmit."

- Persons assigned to the job have no education in the method used for creating a document and its associated quality aspects or they lack knowledge of the domain area. So, they concentrate on headers and numbering schemes, or they point to deliberately blank paragraphs demanding that there should be an entry under every prescribed heading.

- The process model in the company or its organizational structure encourages this kind of behavior by separating the quality assurance people from the actual work of the project.

In more than one organization—usually in large ones—I have found written instructions informing the QA department that its job is to check the completeness, consistency, and formal correctness of documents. But the people assigned to these jobs are not specialists for requirements, design, programming, testing, or any other discipline of system development. They are "QA people." They are supposed to use (tons of) prescribed checklists for (tons of) different kinds of documents and tick them off without looking for the meaning. Process models in such companies often explicitly state that the quality assurance of the content lies with the original authors, those that developed the artifact in the first place. They are supposed to be the specialists in their respective areas.
—PH

An indicator that you are using false quality gates is that the majority of feedback from quality checks is concerned with the form of the deliverable rather than the meaning of the content. The cost of this pattern is the time wasted in unproductive procedures, but more importantly, the cost of the content-related defects that slip through into the final product.

35 Testing Before Testing

"Testing is more than testing (and should start before testing)." —Dorothy Graham

Testing is traditionally done when some of the software has been built. That is, the testers test the delivered code to determine that it is working correctly. Nontraditionally, some organizations distribute their testing activities throughout the life cycle. In particular, they introduce testing during the earliest stages of product development (long before

anything tangible like software is produced), and early in each iteration. Early testing—that is, testing before testing—is done to ensure the project's proposed deliverables *can be* tested for correctness once they have been produced.

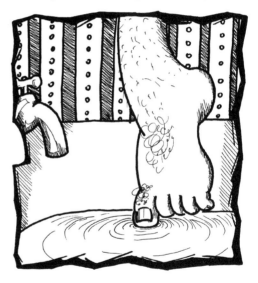

The justification for pre-test testing is that it makes later testing far more productive and, along the way, significantly reduces the amount of time spent correcting avoidable errors. Organizations that use early testing find that later efforts can be safely restricted to testing whether or not the product is working as desired. Many organizations can't do this, because they have little confidence that their definition of "working as desired" is correct. If the requirements themselves have not been tested, then they cannot be trusted by the software testers. The idea of early testing is to provide the later-stage testing with an accurate yardstick against which to measure the solution.

But early testing is not restricted to requirements; it works for any project deliverable. For example, the design of a product can be tested early provided it is communicated in some tangible form. Similarly for the project plans, the scope document, and so on, through the project deliverables. All of these can benefit from early testing when they are presented in a testable form. Additionally, the expectation of early testing influences the producers and results in interim deliverables that are more widely comprehensible.

Belated testing—delaying testing to a time when the product has already been built—cannot help the success of the project. By that stage, if errors exist—and if there is no early testing, they will almost certainly exist—it is too late.

Testing before testing means introducing quality control at the time of the initial project discussions. On projects that do this, the earliest deliverables are tested to see if they make sense before proceeding. The point of this early testing is to uncover as many misconceptions, misunderstandings, conflicts, unrealistic expectations, and so on, as early as possible—before they become entrenched and difficult to dislodge. Testing before testing means you are testing the highest-impact deliverables, which naturally gives you the best return on your testing effort.

36 Cider House Rules

Members of the project team ignore or work around rules made by people who are unconnected to the project's work.

The Cider House Rules, a novel by John Irving, tells the story of a group of apple pickers who return to an orchard every season to pick apples for making cider. During the weeks they pick apples, the pickers live in the old cider house. Inside it, Olive, the owner, has tacked a typewritten page headed Cider House Rules. One of the new pickers, upon reading it, can hardly fail to notice that most of the rules are being openly flouted. Inquiring about these breaches, he is told by a veteran picker, "Nobody pays attention to them rules. Every year Olive writes them up and every year nobody pays no attention."[1]

[1]John Irving, *The Cider House Rules* (New York: William Morrow and Company, 1985), p. 273.

"There are rules, and we do break them."

—Linda Prowse

The problem with the cider house rules is that someone who does not live in the cider house—and has no intention of ever living there—is setting the rules for those who do. Olive lives in the big house and therefore does not appreciate that on hot summer nights, the roof is the only cool place to relax. Nor does she understand that drinking on the roof has become part of the apple pickers' way of life. By setting rules that are inappropriate, she shouldn't be surprised to discover that they are being ignored. By setting rules that are imposed on others from afar, she is asking for them to be defied.

Some development organizations have their own versions of the cider house rules. People who are not involved in project work set the rules for those who are. These organizations have a Process Improvement Office, or a Standards Group, or a Quality Department, whose task is to mandate work processes or methods. These departments might also choose tools to be used by projects or develop standards for the projects' deliverables. These are outsiders setting rules for how a project team should do its work, potentially without any meaningful understanding of that work.

The pattern becomes more apparent when the selection of processes, methods, or tools is the only job of the selector. He does no project work; he just tells those who do the work how they should be doing it.

The outside maker of rules is rarely in the best position to determine how work should be done. When he is not intimately familiar with the work, he generally sets rules that require pointless work to be done. After all, he wants to cover all the bases (including his own rear end), and should things go wrong, his rules must be beyond criticism and absolve him of any blame. Moreover, the rule maker does not want anyone to see his rules as being in any way inadequate.

Naturally, successful project work is not complete anarchy. There must be some rules and defined processes. However, it is necessary for there to be goodness of fit between the world envisioned by the rule makers and the world inhabited by the people who are to follow those rules. The best fit comes when the process or quality specialists are regular members of the project team, or are at least closely aligned with the reality of the project's work. Once this condition is met, the specialists are in the best position to apply their knowledge and define appropriate processes for the team. The burden shifts to the rule maker to be certain that all rules are the right rules for that project.

When the rules are appropriate, the project team will abide by them: They are useful, reasonable, and seen to be sensible. But when reality and rules differ, then reality is king, and you have cider house rules.

37 Talk Then Write

The project team makes decisions during conversations, and then immediately communicates the decisions in writing.

At first reading, this may appear to be nothing more than a statement of the obvious: When you conduct a meeting, you should distribute minutes afterward. We might also conclude it was obvious if we didn't see so many teams operating differently, and suffering for it.

When it comes time to make a decision, you want to do it well and you want to do it quickly. Time is short on development projects. Sometimes, making a decision is on the critical path; resources are blocked, or will soon become blocked, until a decision is reached. More often, decisions are made before they drive the critical path, but they still need to be made quickly, simply because there are so many things to do and so many other decisions to make.

Conversation is the best medium for reaching good decisions quickly. Well-structured conversations bring minds together in an intense, high-bandwidth exchange. You tap the experience and intelligence of multiple team members, over a short period of time, to arrive at a decision that is informed by many perspectives. Unlike meandering e-mail threads, effective conversations work because they are synchronous; parties engage continuously until a decision is reached.

Once a decision is reached, it is time to change gears. You want to communicate the decision you have made, clearly and durably, to all those affected by it. This strategy is hardly new. These are some of the requirements that inspired the Sumerians to invent writing, more than 5,000 years ago. They had long conducted sales and other negotiations through conversation, but they were looking for a more effective way to preserve the results of these commercial and legal transactions. In response, they developed the early writing systems that later evolved into cuneiform.

What worked in the markets and temples of Mesopotamia still has something valuable to offer your twenty-first century projects: Writing persists in a way that memories of conversations do not. Communicating a decision in writing preserves the decision-making conversation for those who were not present and for those who have forgotten its details.

The benefits of intense conversations and clear prose are so obvious that you have to wonder why all teams don't use both methods, selecting whichever one works best in a given situation. A team's communication preferences tend to reflect those of the organization of which it is part, and each organization's culture affects its communication styles. Bigger, more formal organizations tend to rely more on writing. Smaller, more nimble organizations tend to rely more on face-to-face conversations, telephone calls, and less durable forms of writing, such as instant messaging. Teams in such organizations fall into the habit of relying—too much—on whichever form of communication most easily fits their culture.

Teams in small companies often are quite effective at *making* decisions: They have a strong culture of using brief, intense, ad hoc meetings for addressing tough issues and plotting solutions. But their cultures are so rooted in oral communication that they attempt to use this same approach to communicate decisions. They're so comfortable with oral communication that they don't realize when switching gears makes sense.

Failure to switch gears is even easier to see in the case of large companies or distributed teams. When a project team is distributed across large distances, e-mail is often its principal means of communication. Team members can become so comfortable working out of their In boxes that they think nothing of posing a question for decision via e-mail. A dialogue ensues, often with more and more people added to the "CC" line, and what could have been decided in one or two brief meetings stretches across days of debate, without resolution.

The most effective teams have the discipline to employ less culturally comfortable forms of communication when they are the best-suited to the task at hand. Even in the most formal companies, rapid and effective decision-making is done through conversation. And even in the fleetest start-ups, communication of durable decisions is written.

38 Project Sluts

A tendency to take on too much hurts the organization's velocity and results in lowered net effectiveness. But the temptation can be irresistible. . . .

In this era of cost-cutting and staff reductions, there is an emerging consensus—at least among IT professionals—that companies aren't building enough new software, thus missing opportunities for real strategic advantage. If you're part of this consensus, consider for a moment the exact inverse of that idea: Maybe you're building *too much* software.

There seems to be a twenty-first century imperative that everything has to be done yesterday. If speed matters so much, one obvious trade-off is to buy speed by reducing load. This plain, common-sense approach unfortunately flies in the face of an unstated but important political reality: Shedding anything risks offending someone, maybe someone with clout.

Suppose you get a work request from an upper manager, Duane. You know the team is already overloaded, but Duane has clout. He also has a booming voice. If Duane is powerful and loud enough, you may decide to cave.

"Oh, what the hell," you sigh. "Sure, Duane, we'll implement your feature."

Let's go back over that transaction: Your organization has accepted a bit more load than it can comfortably handle. You have done this to stay on the good side of a powerful person. Because the same limited resources now have to be spread over more work, the work on average gets done more slowly. You've essentially sacrificed speed to steer clear of Duane's crosshairs. It gets worse. Duane is not the only powerful person in your company. In fact, anybody who's able to initiate a request for new system work holds some power over you. In your effort to avoid criticism, you may feel compelled to say yes to this work. Each time you say yes, you cause all other work to slow down.

Accepting more work than your team can do well is an act of managerial cowardice. In order to avoid personal criticism, you create conditions in which your team cannot succeed. Ultimately, your team will suffer overwork and lowered esteem in the organization because you did not have the courage to say no in the first place.

What would you have to do to reverse this unfortunate cycle? Prioritize the work and do only as much as you can handle at maximum speed. Put lower-value work on hold until higher-value work is completed.

This may be difficult to implement. You're delivering value faster, but you're giving up clout. As you say no to powerful people, your effectiveness increases but your political power may drop. The underlying principle here is not comforting: You can get more essential work done faster, but only by foregoing some potential political power.

Politics is not the only reason organizations overload themselves. Individuals are similarly inclined to let themselves become overburdened. They can't say no. They've heard that less is more, but in their hearts they know that only *more is more.*

Taking on more than you can handle at maximum speed is a recipe for getting slow. You almost never see the quantity/speed tradeoff stated quite this bluntly—it's downright unappealing. Its lack of appeal helps explain why so many organizations are slowed almost to a stop by the sheer quantity of work they're trying to get done. If they paused to separate the wheat from the chaff, they would realize that what's slowing them down is *so much chaff.*

If you're a manager, allowing this pattern to persist (either by your actions or those of your subordinates) puts your project at substantial and unnecessary risk.

39 Atlas

The team's leader excels at (almost) everything.

You love visiting Erica's team. She runs a development team of about twenty-five people, and it is one of the best in the company. They ship great products. They hit their dates. Many of the best, young, new hires want to work for Erica, so she has her pick of the top talent when there are openings. But openings are few because team members tend to stay a long time. They come because they know they will learn a lot. They stay because, over time, Erica helps them develop their technical skills, from the most basic to the most elite.

It doesn't take much insight to see that this success is due in large part to Erica's leadership. She does everything for her team. She drives product planning and the development of release schedules, and she takes part in most architectural decisions. If some of the junior developers fall behind toward the end of a release cycle, Erica will jump right in and help them finish on time.

Erica is just as effective in dealing with the corporate side of things. When it comes time for performance reviews and salary planning, Erica would rather do them herself than impose such administrative work on her hard-working leads. When her team needs to coordinate efforts with teams at other sites, Erica is their ambassador. In fact, most of the people at other development sites have never met anyone from Erica's site other than Erica.

You love visiting Erica's team, but you wish that things could be different.

Erica is doing just about everything you could want from a leader, except one. By being the total leader and manager, she is not leaving any significant leadership or management work for her team-mates to do. She is, as a consequence, not cultivating them as leaders.

Consider what a team like Erica's looks like structurally. She has a total of twenty-five people divided into smaller sub-teams. There are several teams of developers, a team or two of testers, and a couple of technical writers, as well as two or three individual contributors in various specialties. Each of the smaller teams has a team lead. If they've been chosen well, these team leads are the Ericas of the future. Some, of course, will not want to move up as managers. They may wish to stay at a level where they can remain at the technical leading edge. But some will see something of themselves in Erica, or in the managers above her. To follow in her path, they need the initial opportunity to do a small part of Erica's job, so they can learn her whole job, one piece at a time. By insisting on owning every aspect of leadership and management, Erica is starving potential leaders of essential learning experiences. She loves them, but she's stunting their growth.

We've already enumerated the many significant virtues of Erica's team and those like it. Let's consider the other consequences of her leadership style. The most obvious has already been stated: Potential leaders are not developed as leaders. But there are two other consequences that may not be immediately apparent.

First, Erica's model does not scale very well. Erica probably started by leading a group of four-to-six developers. She managed each individual directly. By her intelligence, skill, and drive, she has come to the point where she is leading a very high-performing team of twenty-five, divided into, say, five smaller teams. On the org chart, Erica manages the team leads, and they manage the team members. But when you take into account her style of leadership, it becomes clear that although she may have five team leads, she is still managing all twenty-five individuals directly.

When a challenge comes along that requires a team of one hundred, can her boss look to Erica to lead that new team? Almost certainly not. While an extraordinarily talented first-line leader like Erica can succeed with a team of twenty-five, her methods will not work on a team of one hundred. As effective as Erica's style is in the small, managers who are limited to it cannot take on large assignments.

Second, what if Erica is suddenly gone? Who steps in? Who takes over the team and enables it to continue such fine performance? If you are Erica's manager, you are now very worried. You have exactly one realistic option, and it is inherently risky: You need to bring in a new leader from outside the team. You will either have to hire from outside, or you will have to redeploy one of your other managers. Either way, the new leader has a tough road ahead.

Erica's team has been completely imprinted on Erica. It will be a major challenge for a new leader to win quick acceptance. In addition, the new leader cannot be expected to do a perfect imitation of Erica's style, which means that he or she will now have to call upon the team leads to do more of the work of leadership and management than they have previously been expected to do. If the new leader is very fortunate, some of these team leads will rise to these higher expectations and quickly grow into the leaders they always had the potential to become. If not, some of the team leads themselves will have to be replaced, further traumatizing the organization, just as it's reeling from the departure of the manager who did (almost) everything for them.

40 Everyone Wears Clothes for a Reason

A policy of total openness makes progress grind to a stop.

Organizations that consider themselves "open" are usually pretty pleased to be so. They brag, "We're an open shop here," and expect others to be properly impressed. But there is a downside to too much openness, nicely expressed by intelligence studies pioneer Herb Simon: "An abundance of information creates a paucity of attention."[1] When the ratio of information to attention gets high enough, we're in overload. More information doesn't help.

---

[1]H.A. Simon, "Designing Organizations for an Information-Rich World," in *The Economics of Communication and Information*, D.M. Lamberton, ed., (Cheltenham, U.K.: Edward Elgar, 1997), pp. 187–203.

At one smallish IT organization I consult for, all staff members are routinely invited to all meetings. What's worse is that they all often attend. You might wonder why. One of the managers explained the rationale: "What you have to understand about this organization, Tom, is that everybody feels they need to know everything in order to do anything."

—TDM

If everyone needs to know everything to get anything done in your organization, you're toast.

The opposite of a totally open organization would be one in which you had access to information only on a need-to-know basis. This would be typical of a high-security environment, such as defense planning or weapons development. Such organizations are a bit inconvenienced by the rigorous closing down of access, but they can nonetheless function. They are probably more functional than the totally open organization.

Obviously, the middle ground between these two extremes is where you want to be. It's nice to feel that you'd be welcome to learn some of the particulars of a project going on nearby. This bit of openness suggests that your personal growth is acknowledged by the organization as something it should want to facilitate. But openness is a quality that needs not to be maximized.

It's not enough to note that too much information can be a bad thing. The larger issue is to understand why we burden ourselves with too much in the first place. One reason is that information offered by others may come with Faustian strings attached: If you receive some information and don't complain about it, you in effect agree to whatever it says. (See Pattern 25, "Silence Gives Consent.")

A more common reason we burden ourselves with information is information anxiety—the fear of not knowing what others know. If you give in to this, you're like the kid at his first wedding buffet—you load up on everything that looks good, for fear of missing any taste experience. Learning how much will fit on your information plate is more than just good strategy, it's part of growing up.

41 Peer Preview

The organization involves peers of the candidate in the hiring process.

In most organizations today, the ultimate decision to offer a candidate a technical position lies clearly with management. Managers hire, and managers fire; no doubt about it. But in some organizations, the decision of whether to offer positions to technical people rests—in part—with those who will be their colleagues. This *peer preview* has only one outcome: When managers let the technical staff have a say, everyone—candidate, staff, and manager—comes out ahead.

The early stages of the hiring process are pretty much unchanged: There is an initial screening of the candidate's credentials, most often by the front-line manager. The manager may ask a senior technical staff member to review the résumés and divide them into Next-Step and No-Thanks piles. The manager may have preliminary telephone conversations with the candidates who look best on paper, to determine which of them to invite for an in-person interview. The invited candidates are told to expect to spend anywhere from three to six hours meeting the team. When colleagues participate in the hiring process, the interview day is typically a long one.

After an invited candidate arrives and is greeted by the manager, the candidate begins the first in a series of interviews with individual team members, with meetings lasting from thirty to ninety minutes.

Although peer-preview interviewers seek the same kind of information about the candidate, each goes about the quest in a different way. Obviously, everyone wants to assess the candidate's knowledge, skills, and abilities. And so, depending on the type of position to be filled, the group as a whole may ask the candidate to write some code or to build a test set. But each interviewer will also assess the candidate as a person, asking himself: "Can I work with this person?" "Will he fit into our team?" "Will he make our team stronger or weaker?"

In addition, individual interviewers evaluate the candidate based on their own role on the team. If, for example, the candidate is a developer, an interviewer who is a tester will ask different questions, and look for different traits, than will a fellow developer.

Each interviewer also assesses the candidate based on his own past experiences, asking himself questions like these: "Does this person exhibit the skills and problem-solving styles that I have come to value most?" "To what extent does this person remind me of past teammates with whom I have worked well, or with whom I have not been able to succeed?" "Is this person as good as he seems or is he a fake?" The diversity of backgrounds among interviewers enables the team to screen prospective members from a variety of perspectives and values.

After an interviewer hands the candidate off to a peer, he confers with the manager—in person, by e-mail, by telephone—about his impressions and opinions of the candidate. Each staffer gets to cast an if-it-were-only-up-to-me-would-I-hire-this-person vote.

If all has gone well in the interviews, the candidate is brought back to the manager, who by now has been briefed by the interviewers. The manager is now in position to conduct his own interview and then to inform the candidate if an offer will be forthcoming. The manager might find cause not to make an offer to a candidate whom the other interviewers found acceptable, but it makes no sense to hire a candidate if a significant portion of the team has given thumbs down.

When the team has a real say in the hiring process, everyone wins:

- The existing team members win because the day the new hire walks through the door, many of them have already met him, and in effect, have endorsed him; those that the staff could not accept never cross the threshold.
- The candidate wins because he is in a better position to decide whether he wants to join this team. He gets to meet his prospective peers, not just the boss. He can ask about real life on the job. He can smell the corporate culture.
- The manager wins because he can rely on his team for a technical evaluation of the candidate rather than surmise it on his own. He also knows that the team has to some extent already accepted the new guy and has a stake in his success.
- Finally, the team as a whole wins because team members learn from each other as they go through the peer-preview process. When reading others' evaluations of the candidate, team members discover questions and criteria that they can apply to future candidates. And the manager learns more about how his own team members think.

Speaking of managers, peer previews are equally useful for hiring team leaders. Why not ask some members of the team to interview those who might become their boss?

Whether the candidate is a developer, a tester, or a manager, finding a really good person is never easy, but always important. It's a team project.

"Managing is getting paid for home runs someone else hits."
—Casey Stengel

42 Snorkeling and Scuba Diving

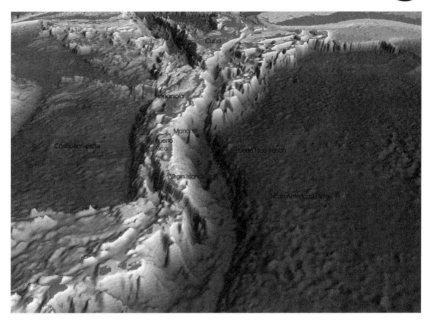

Analysis activities continue through the life of the project: top-down, bottom-up, and middle-every-which-way.[1]

A snorkeler swimming across the surface of the water sees fish swimming in the shallows and the shadows of creatures in the depths. A scuba diver goes farther below the surface of the water; he makes deeper dives and investigates the shadows to discover details of the fish, wrecks, and coral in a specific area. Given the same amount of time, snorkelers cover more breadth; scuba divers, more depth. Successful project teams make effective use of time by combining the skills of snorkeling and scuba diving throughout the project and by making reasoned choices about which approach to take, when.

Snorkeling is a fine technique that project teams can use to discover how much area needs investigation in order to understand the problem and meet the goal. Typically, at the start of a project or sub-

---

[1]Thanks to Dines Hansen for inspiring the pattern statement.

project, snorkeling identifies the scope of the investigation, the goals, the stakeholders, the boundaries of the investigation, what is already known, and where some scuba diving needs to be done.

The diver makes a deep scuba dive when he suspects there is something interesting to see, something new, or some deeper detail. A deep dive often yields discoveries that change assumptions made while snorkeling. Suppose we discover a species of marine life we didn't expect to find in these waters; then we'll need to make a wider investigation to find the species' breeding ground.

An indication of this pattern is when a team takes a wide (snorkel) view in parallel with—not instead of—doing selected, detailed (scuba) work. What's key is the ability to apply *wide* and *deep* investigatory skills throughout the project. The width of the investigation identifies people, organizations, hardware, and software systems that might have some effect on the project. Increasing knowledge about the width identifies the areas of highest risk and greatest benefit, areas that would provide profit from a deeper investigation.

Project teams that snorkel and scuba dive are not daunted by a wide scope. Team members know they do not need to investigate the entire scope to the same depth. For example, if they decide to buy a solution for part of the scope, then the depth of that investigation is only as much as is needed to fit the work situation to the capabilities of the solution. When they intend to build their own solution, they make judgments on what depth of investigation is necessary for the proposed changes. They also know that some of the deeper investigation can be deferred to a more convenient time. Project teams with a wide scope are better able to respond to changes because they can see the ramifications of the change. They know what they know and what they don't know, what they need to explore and what they can leave alone. They can plan how to use resources to their best advantage.

Projects that snorkel and scuba dive are highly likely to use prototypes and simulations in conjunction with context modeling. They are also likely to incrementally deliver the most beneficial functionality early in the project. Also, they are able to coherently explain the scope and goals of the project in one page.

The opposite of this pattern is when a team is either addicted to detail ("We only do scuba diving—none of that sissy snorkeling") or scared of detail ("We're snorkelers—in other words, afraid of sea monsters"). You will also spot the opposite when people talk about "high level" and "detail" as if these are separate things that don't need to have any traceable relationship.

Good developers do not limit themselves: They can snorkel and scuba dive. They choose the technique depending on what they need to see. When reconnoitering, a shallow dive will suffice, but inspecting necessitates a deeper dive.

Sometimes, just dipping your toe in the water is enough to tell you not to plunge in.

43 It's Always the Goddamned Interfaces

Project team members focus relentlessly on interfaces, both automated and human.

In order to design a system, we must know the interfaces between the system and the environment. We need to know the system's raw inputs and its final products. Until we have that census of inputs and outputs, we are in preliminary analysis: We have not bounded the problem. Once we have that census, we can start to define the functionality of the system.

What happens in design, after we get agreement on functionality? We break a large, complex system into subsystems, and subsystems into components. And yes, a useful way to confine these subsystems and components is to enumerate in turn each of their unique inputs and outputs.

How do we divide the work of implementation? By subsystem and/or by component. A team may take a subsystem to work on, and individuals will build and test components. The subsystem and component boundaries define the edge of the work, the exact responsibility of each developer. These interfaces are contracts between components; one says to another, "You give me exactly this data, only under these conditions, and I will create precisely this product, to be stored in that specific location."

In the early stages of the project, before you have dug into all the minute details, declaring an interface with implementable exactitude can be very difficult, and it can be even more difficult to realize that a nuance has gone unnoticed. Clearly, leaving any interface undefined is no solution at all, so we must define each, to the best of our understanding at the time.

All this adds up to the strong possibility of having interface defects that impact at least two—and probably more—components, and are usually the toughest to deal with.

Teams that know this pattern attack the interfaces early. They build threads of code that exercise interfaces before they have committed to all the components' code. They integrate individuals' code early, and they test often.

> *We met with a single project that had three work groups—one in Canada, one in the U.S., and one in Israel. The manager had on the project intranet a document he called "the Interface Bible." It was the sole document of record of all system interfaces; anything else about any interface was irrelevant. He swore by his bible, so he didn't need to swear about the goddamned interfaces.*
>
> —TRL

Managers who know this pattern pay attention to the interfaces of the project team, battling the possibility that any group could be making false assumptions about any interface. Remember Conway's Law: *The product will reflect the organizational structure that produced it.* This is particularly true of the interfaces: Complex human interfaces on the project are liable to result in complex product interfaces.

44 The Blue Zone

"Orville Wright didn't have a pilot's license."
—Richard Tait, Grand Poo Bah, Cranium

The team has at least one member who routinely exceeds authorization.

Meet Winston. Winston typifies a certain personality that you encounter from time to time on development projects. He's not quite an anarchist, but he seems to report only to himself. He appears to do pretty much what he sees as best for the project, regardless of his marching orders. And yet, he never really goes too far. He just stretches his authority—and sometimes his manager's patience—near to the breaking point. Winston operates in the blue zone.

When a manager hands out assignments, he sets boundaries such that the recipient has enough latitude to achieve the objectives of the assignment, while taking into account the team member's abilities. The manager also tries to prevent different assignments from overlapping or colliding.

Thoughtful task definition establishes a wide lane within which the assigned team member may operate freely. However, it is almost impossible to specify exactly everything that needs to be done as part of the assignment. We think of project assignments as creating three zones of authorization:

- The green zone consists of the things that are explicitly a part of the assignment: the core of the work to be done.
- The red zone includes anything that is explicitly excluded from the scope of the assignment.
- The blue zone is everything else: activities that are neither required nor prohibited by the assignment. In other words, everything that lies between the green and red zones.

Our colleague Winston believes that he can do anything that he has not been explicitly told not to do. Not only will he carry out the assignment as stated (his green zone), but he also feels he should do anything in the blue zone he thinks needs to be done to achieve the best outcome. His only criterion for acting is that whatever he does must be beneficial to his project. He doesn't wait for permission; he doesn't ask for it. He just does whatever he thinks needs to be done.

There is more to Winston. We sometimes see him attempting to persuade the team leader to let him operate in the red zone. Permission to do what he has been told explicitly not to do is the only permission he seeks.

Having a Winston on your team is a real benefit. Although life with him can be hair-raising, he gets things done. And his adventurous nature means he often comes up with better and more-innovative solutions than those envisioned by the original assignment.

Winston looks especially valuable when you consider Benson, his polar opposite. Benson is the fastidious team member who assumes that unless he has been specifically told to do something, he must ask for permission before doing anything. For Benson, the blue zone is out of bounds. Regardless of the value of doing so, he ventures there rarely and only after asking explicit permission.

Because he has been told not to venture into the red zone, Benson sees this prohibition as both everlasting and beyond questioning. He might even stand by and watch the project fail rather than suggest a solution that lies in the red zone, far beyond the scope of his formal assignment.

Both Benson and Winston personify paradoxes: One shows that strict obedience can be harmful; the other demonstrates the potential value of some benevolent anarchy.

"The correct amount of anarchy on a project is not zero."
—Mike Mushet

45 News Improvement

"We can't possibly make January"	"We're frankly worried about January"	"January will be a challenge, Sir, but ..."	"I can confidently report that January is AOK"
Team Leader	Project Manager	Applications Manager	CIO

Bad news is not conveyed accurately upward through the organization.

In some organizations, bad news does not get reported upward at all. More often, bad news is improved as it travels upward from one level to the next. Consider the example shown above.

News improvement is a destructive pattern because it deprives decision-makers of needed information, and this can lead to bad decisions (or missed decisions) and outcomes that are worse than they need be. There are many famous examples of bad decisions that could have been avoided had information flowed more effectively. In the last quarter-century, perhaps the decision to launch the space shuttle Challenger on January 28, 1986, is the best illustration of this pattern.

According to author Diane Vaughan in her book *The Challenger Launch Decision,*[1] engineers from Morton-Thiokol recommended against the launch due to concerns about the cold-weather performance of O-ring seals between the sections of the solid rocket motors. After Marshall Space Flight Center officials criticized Thiokol for its recommendation, senior Thiokol managers reversed the recommendation of their engineers and approved the launch. The fact that Thiokol had initially recommended against launching in cold weather was not relayed by the Marshall managers to the senior NASA program manager. The decision to proceed with the launch in unusually cold weather led to the deaths of the crew and the destruction of the spacecraft.

[1]Diane Vaughan, *The Challenger Launch Decision: Risky Technology, Culture, and Deviance at NASA* (Chicago: The University of Chicago Press, 1996).

Thankfully, not all instances of news improvement have such tragic consequences. When you see this pattern in projects, the most typical symptom is surprise, and the typical consequences are missed deadlines and expectations that aren't met.

Project surprises often follow a story like this: After a few months of development, with successful interim deliverables along the way, the new system is slated for the final round of testing, with shipment in about a month. After a planning session for the last development activities, the project manager reports that an additional month of work will be needed before the system will be ready to ship. Needless to say, the senior managers who hear this are appalled. How could the team get so close to the scheduled completion date before realizing that it was not going to make it?

The usual answer is that many members of a team know much earlier that the deadline is unrealistic. They may say so to their supervisors, or even express concerns in their own status reports. But somewhere between the front line and the senior managers, their disbelief in the project's schedule is filtered out of the project's stream of reports.

Suppressing bad news can turn solvable problems into unsolvable problems. The few people who might be able to do something about a surprise slip—the senior managers who control the resources and who set external expectations for the project—are deprived of the opportunity to take corrective action until so late in the process that all options for corrective action have expired. Had they known early enough about the imbalance between the work to be done and the resources and time available, they could have provided more resources or re-scoped the effort or extended the schedule early enough to avoid last-minute slippage. It's not certain that they *would* have fixed the problem if they had heard the bad news immediately, but it is certain that they *cannot* fix a problem that they never hear about. Early warning is essential.

So, why does this happen? The most common cause is fear. No one enjoys hearing bad news about the people and things they care about. Quite often, managers allow their normal human dislike of bad news to affect their reaction to it, and more importantly, their treatment of those who report it. "Don't shoot the messenger" is the mantra we invoke against this behavior, but it often doesn't work. If an organization's management culture—by its actions more than its words—

makes it clear that bearers of bad news will suffer, news improvement becomes inevitable.

There is at least one other type of management-induced news improvement. Team members typically *know* the project is in trouble long before they can *prove* it. In some cultures, a team member who declares a problem with meeting a target date is likely to be met with the famous line, "How do you know for sure that you *can't* make it?" Not wanting to be viewed as whiners or cowards, team members say nothing until calamity is inarguable (and often, inevitable).[2]

What can you do to improve your organization's ability to quickly and accurately convey bad news upwardly? Most of the solution falls to you, the manager. You not only have to *declare* that you want to hear bad news immediately, you have to *behave* that way. At the very least, this means separating your reaction to bad news into two components: (1) determining what to do about it, and (2) figuring out how it happened. Focus first on the former. Don't immediately dive into an investigation of why whatever went wrong happened. Instead, concentrate on enabling your team, including the bearer of the bad news, to come up with a "get well" plan and to put it into action. Your emphasis on constructive corrective action is less likely to be viewed as criticism or punishment by your organization, and therefore, it is less likely to cause people to suppress or distort bad news in the future. Eventually, you do need to do a root-cause analysis so similar mishaps can be avoided, but this can wait until the situation has been corrected. By that time, people generally feel much less defensive, and bad news can be addressed rather than improved.

---

[2]See also Pattern 46, "Telling the Truth Slowly."

46 Telling the Truth Slowly

Corporate culture pressures people into withholding discomforting information.

In 1994, President Bill Clinton named Mike McCurry as his press secretary. At that time, McCurry was already well known to the members of the press corps. In his first press conference, a reporter asked him, "You won't lie to us as press secretary now, will you?" McCurry responded, "No, but, I'd tell the truth slowly."

Project managers and team members sometimes end up telling the truth slowly for reasons such as the following:

- They don't want to own the problem they announce. Many cultures send out the message that if you're the one who notices a mess, you get to clean it up:

  > "Gee, Boss, we could have major performance problems now that we are tripling the number of concurrent users on that old backbone system."
  >
  > "You're right, Smithers. Make sure that doesn't happen."

- They don't have an answer to the follow-up question they know they will get. Stating a problem without an immediate remedy to propose is considered whining, and whiners are career-limited in many organizations.

  > "Gee, Boss, this project might be late."
  > "How late, Smithers?"
  > "Gee, Boss, I don't know."
  > "Whiner," Boss mumbles under his breath.

- They are waiting for someone else to reveal a bigger problem that they can hide their own problems behind. This comes from the Someone-Else-Will-Flinch-First School of Career Management.

  > "I've called this meeting of all Team Leads on the project because Smithers here has informed me that his group is at least two months behind schedule. He isn't exactly sure," here the Boss sighs, "so, to be safe, I will officially postpone delivery for four months."
  >
  > The Team Leads say out loud, "That's too bad, Smithers. Well, we can always use the extra time for more testing. Smithers, want the new guy in Ralph's group to help you out?"

  That's what the Team Leads say; what they really mean is

  > "Smithers broke! We knew he was a wussie and a whiner. We hope these four more months will cover our own unannounced slippages."

If Smithers can survive long enough, he will learn that telling the truth quickly is the path to martyrdom. He will learn that his organization doesn't want the immediate truth; it wants happiness for as long as it can have it. He will observe that the truth will eventually tell out, but the organization prefers to "deal with it" when that day comes. Until that day, Smithers, now a team player, will tell the truth s—l—o—w—l—y.

> Hiding your problems behind those of others is sometimes called "Schedule Chicken."

47 Practicing Endgame

The team measures its emerging product against the release criteria at regular intervals during development.

It's your first day of a new course of study. Your instructor greets you and the other students and then proceeds to describe how he plans to conduct the class. He concludes by saying, "I don't believe in waiting until the end of the semester to give the final exam. I prefer to give it every two weeks throughout the term. Of course, it won't be the same final exam each time, but it will cover the same material in more or less the same way."

This may sound wacky, but it's pretty similar to what we mean by "practicing endgame."

To understand the appeal of this approach, let's contrast it against what happens on all-too-many software projects: the Readiness Review Folk Dance. It usually proceeds in several movements:

- *Procrastination during the definition of release criteria:* "Well, the ship date is months away, and the Readiness Review occurs just a week or so before the planned ship date—and there are really urgent things to do right now!"

- *The pre-review fire drill:* "Ohmygod, the review is in less than two weeks! Where did we put those release criteria? How are we doing against them? Gosh, how would we measure this one?"

- *The solemn Readiness Review ceremony:* Everyone knows that the review happens so close to the ship date that any significant problems will cause the team to miss the date— "There isn't enough time left to do any serious fixing." So, everyone realizes that the only acceptable declaration is, "Ready to ship." Too many defects? Service pack!

- *The post-review fire drill:* After the ceremony is declared a success, a few worried people gather to figure out which of the most heinous gaps in the release criteria can be cured by the ship date without doing more harm than good.

- *The lessons unlearned lament:* No one enjoyed this. Everyone vows to do better next time. Unfortunately, next time is months away, and we've got to get started on the next release, because there are really urgent things to do right now!

Like most folk dances, this one varies from one team culture to another, but we suspect that you recognize one or two aspects of your own variant in this description.

Teams that practice endgame develop their release criteria early in the project. They then develop whatever tests are required to assess the product's fulfillment of the criteria. These tests are run at the completion of every development iteration, followed by a brief Readiness Review.

Consider the benefits of this approach:

- At every stage of development, your team becomes refocused on the work left to do in order to ship the product.
- You get early warning of regressions against criteria that were previously met.
- You have multiple opportunities to refine your release criteria as you go.

This can be an awkward process. Some release criteria are very difficult to measure meaningfully early in development. Nevertheless, even those big black "TBDs" prompt useful questions like, "Hey, when *are* we going to run the performance suite for the first time?"

48 The Music Makers

People with musical skills are disproportionately represented, sometimes extremely so, in information technology organizations.

We admit that we don't know what proportion of the population in modern society can play a musical instrument, so we are (pun intended) singing in the dark. However, we are convinced that we can see a pattern: There is an oddly large number of musicians in the information technology industry, and they seem to congregate pronouncedly within some organizations.

Over the course of a year, each of us at the Atlantic Systems Guild comes into contact with dozens of IT organizations. Casual questioning always turns up a surprising number of musical folks within the ranks of the people we deal with—more than the number of musicians we meet in everyday life. This might be rooted in the mathematical and logical foundations of music, and how it appeals to the more technologically minded. It might be the wonderful contrast between the digital nature of the technology and the analog nature of the music itself. Or it might just be a coincidence.

We also find that some organizations are awash in musical talent. The following stories are representative.

> *My favorite example of this is the Landmark Graphics annual software meeting where all the software project people meet to talk about what they have been doing for the last year. Some of the meeting time is not managed by the conference committee; this is time for music, singing, and dancing, all by the employees. There are bands everywhere in the hotel, and if you aren't in one, you can roam the corridors to find the music you like. The bands are really good. Some Landmark musicians told me that sometimes it's a challenge to rehearse because the drummer is in Calgary and the rest of the band is in Houston. Despite the difficulties, they manage to come together and play some mean music on the big night at the annual meeting.*
>
> —TRL

Borys Stokalski of Infovide-Matrix (that's him singing at the microphone in this pattern's photo) told us this story:

> *"Late night in corporate offices of Infovide-Matrix, the lights are still on. One could think of yet another desperate story of meeting an impossible deadline, or completing a slide show for next day's important customer presentation. But this story is about fun, friendship, and . . . some noise. Wojtek, the IT director of a bank, is fixing his drum kit. Lukasz, a bright software-quality consultant, tries a new riff on his bass, while Pawel, a great project manager, is tuning his beloved Gibson Les Paul Supreme. Aidan, an alliance manager of a major software vendor, has still not arrived, but when he does, his alto sax will add some great tones to the stuff they are going to try out this night. Grego, manager of the IT Governance competence center, and I discuss the details of guitar arrangement—having three guitars on stage requires some planning, to avoid sound clutter. We practice and perform whenever there is an occasion for a small gig—for the sheer fun of music and stage performance. This is the genre of After Hours Rock."*

In Silicon Valley, Vittorio Viarengo, vice president of development at Oracle, also leads Jam4Dinner, an all-software-industry combo that performs as both a trio and a quintet. Several of the band's recordings are available on its Website.

Try asking around your organization and see how many of your coworkers are musicians. We cannot guarantee you will find a complete orchestra, but you will probably be able to put together a string quartet or a rock band. Our iPods await the result.

49 Journalists

Journalists are project managers who detach the goal of accurate reporting from the goal of project success.

Project managers know that they have to understand the true state of their projects and to report accurately on them. Sometimes, however, they lose sight of the reason for all this attention to detail: to make sure the project achieves its objectives. They adopt as their goal the accurate portrayal of the state of the project at all times. They become, in effect, journalists. Like film critics,[1] project journalists believe—if only subconsciously—that they can succeed even if their project fails.

Consider the situation of a journalist reporting on a plane crash. The journalist feels accountable for reporting accurately which plane crashed, when and where it crashed, how many people were onboard, and whether any of them survived. The journalist does not feel guilty for not having prevented the crash. That was someone else's job.

---

[1]See Pattern 19, "Film Critics."

Journalist project managers come across the same way. Their reports are models of clarity, accuracy, and detail. They know exactly how late the Order Entry subsystem is, by how many days it is pushing out the critical path, and how that will affect dependent downstream tasks. But they have lost sight of something pretty important: Their roles *exist* to ensure that their projects have happy endings. Just as the pilot's primary goal is to avoid killing all the passengers, the project manager is first and foremost supposed to ensure that the project "lands" at the right destination, safely and on-time. Accurate reporting along the way is one means to achieve these goals, but it is no substitute for them.

50 The Empty Chair

No individual is accountable for the conceptual integrity of the entire user experience.

Some time ago, I was working with a company developing security systems. The company's new product generation was to have speech input and output in addition to the touch-screen interface on its line of small devices. Therefore, management had set up two user-interface teams: one responsible for the touch screens and one responsible for the audio interface. These two teams were located in different cities working off their feature lists without ever questioning the overall business process that the devices were meant to support. Looking at the project from the outside, one could immediately see that more discussion between the two would have led to a far better use of the two technologies.

—JSR

Imagine that your company is awarded a new development contract and that you are appointed as project manager. You feel capable of doing the job since you have all the required skills and experience. You distribute the work according to the different skills needed, either among departments in your company or between your own departments and a partner

company that is specialized in one of the relevant technical domains. You have capable subproject managers, and they take up their assignments with enthusiasm.

The subproject teams are content with the work allocated to them, they understand the goals of the overall project, and they do a fantastic job in their domain. They do come back to you, but only for more time or money or other resource-related project issues. Your sub-teams work in different geographical areas, but you are not worried since the distribution of work among the teams is well documented. They formally cooperate with each other, negotiate interfaces, and share their intermediate results.

The customer offers excellent domain input for the subject matter, but different domain experts are assigned to the different subprojects. And sometimes these domain experts do not even know who among their colleagues is working on the other part of the same project.

At the helm of the project, you and the top manager from the customer organization work closely together to manage expectations and to track the progress of the many sub-teams.

And yet, your project is almost certain to yield a product that does not work very well in the eyes of its users. What's wrong?

Your project has left one chair empty. Many projects fall short of real success for want of a single individual whose responsibility it is to ensure that the resulting business process—from the users' points of view—works as well as possible. This person is interested in the best output of the overall project for the customer's business—down to the finest details.

We're not talking about a project manager, nor are we talking about the overall leader of the project team. This person may not have any direct reports, and he almost certainly is not also accountable for budget or schedule. His entire focus is on how the product will interact with its target environment, especially its users.

Such persons carry all manner of job titles: product manager, system architect, business analyst, and so on. Some call themselves technical project managers since their job is to care about the details of the solution (in contrast with the overall project manager, who handles budgets, staff, and schedules). Regardless of the title, these people are not part of any sub-team; they work across all sub-teams.

It may be sufficient to have such a person only on the customer side. If somebody from the customer's organization constantly questions the synergy of the subproject, you may succeed, even if the teams on the contractor's side lack any similar unifying role.

The empty chair is even more often found in projects chartered to integrate already existing products. Here, the technical aspects of integration drive the project while details of business integration, ergonomics of user interaction, and creative ideas that could lead to breakthrough synergies are ignored.

Take a look around your project team's table. Is there an empty chair?

51 My Cousin Vinny

Team members argue—vigorously and without rancor—to appraise and improve their ideas.

Soon after humans started using language, they started arguing. Not every argument since that time has been beneficial; many have been of very dubious advantage to the proponents. Nevertheless, throughout history, well-intentioned people have used argument and debate to validate ideas—often improving them while doing so.

Team members argue over their ideas and proposals all the time. They use argument as a way to explore their ideas and to arrive at a consensus on what to do. If the arguments for an idea are unconvincing, then the idea is unlikely to be adopted. However, should skeptics become convinced during the argument, they almost certainly will become enthusiastic advocates for the idea. If, during the course of the argument, flaws appear in the idea, given time, teammates usually turn to repairing them. While an idea is being debated, the cut and thrust of the argument is almost guaranteed to generate new ones.

Film still from Jonathan Lynn's 1992 movie, *My Cousin Vinny:* On the stand, Mona Lisa Vito argues with lawyer Vincent Gambini. From elsewhere in the movie: "Stan, listen to me. You have to see the Gambinis in action. I mean, these people, they love to argue. I mean, they live to argue."

The point of arguing is to convince others, and while we are doing so, to convince ourselves. If you want to convince someone else, then of necessity, your ideas must be well formed and articulated. In other words, you have to think about them a little more and consider whether the idea will withstand the spirited—and public—scrutiny it is about to receive. We would all like to come across as knowledgeable whilst arguing, and so take more care to ensure we are presenting a rational, well-crafted idea.

The eponymous hero of this pattern won his court case through clever argument. His presentation of the case and his arguments against those of the prosecution were enough to convince the jury. Similarly, beneficial arguing in projects is not the usual bickering and disputes that go on in most offices—whose football team is the best, Mac versus Windows, and so on. It's the meaty discussion that advances the system being built. Which design best fits the requirements? What level of security provides the best safety for stored information, yet allows the degree of needed access? And, should preventing accidental misuse by authorized users have a higher priority than preventing intrusion from outside agents since the former is more common? These, like many issues that confront a project team, are multifaceted and need to be aired and argued over if the best end-result is to emerge.

Some arguments are on a grand scale—the proponents are determining the overall look and feel of the product. The marketing people argue for a cool, uncluttered appearance; the usability expert argues for enough visible controls to make common tasks simple to do; the developers argue for pet features and against anything they think will result in an inelegant implementation.

> Some arguments are about smaller-scale, but nevertheless important, issues. I sat spellbound through an argument about the best way of reducing the number of instructions in a disk access routine. Bizarrely, the proponents of this argument chose to sit on their desks and talk over the partitions of their adjoining cubicles.
>
> —JSR

Team members who argue in their search for better solutions respect each other—it is often safe to say they like each other. Otherwise, they cannot have productive argument. When an argument is flowing, team members know that the discussion and dissection of their idea is not an attack on them; it's merely an attempt to deliver the best product in an efficient manner. But this kind of safety does not come from benevolent management or well-meaning team leaders. It comes from within: The team members know that argument is not personal, that it is not to establish a pecking order or to showcase a tiresome display of personal knowledge. It comes from knowing that other guy is your cousin Vinny. He is testing your ideas and attempting to advance them—by arguing with you.

52 Feature Soup

"Beautiful Soup, so rich and green,
Waiting in a hot tureen!
Who for such dainties would not stoop?
Soup of the evening, beautiful Soup!"

　　　　　—Lewis Carroll, *Alice's Adventures in Wonderland*

The product sports a superabundance of piecemeal features, many of which do little to address the customer's real business needs.

It starts innocently. One of the marketing staff has a request from a customer to add an extra pull-down menu. Then a requirement arrives to add an export interface to the product, the product manager wants to include a new analysis report, and the DBA asks for another new field in the database and to change the color of the background. All of these requirements, and many more, are passed to the developers for inclusion in the product. The features of the product grow with each addition, but after a while, everyone—marketing, customers, and development—loses sight of how all these pieces fit together and how they  help achieve the business goals. The project that once set out with the intention of meeting a specific purpose has instead become an indigestible soup of unconnected features.

　　　　The situation becomes soupier because each of the interested parties views the product's requirements very differently and there is no common, connective thread. Marketing groups each collection of requirements as a marketable feature—not necessarily with any functional cohesion. The developers group the requirements according to the implementation technology they are using. Each customer thinks of the requirements in terms of the individual fragments of his own work. The impact of these unconnected requirements is that nobody has a consistent way to talk about progress or to make decisions about changes. It becomes impossible to make trade-offs in terms of the themes of a product release because there are no coherent themes; instead, the product becomes a bag of miscellaneous tricks.

So, why do so many products end up as feature soup? It starts with the sources of the requirements—people.

People naturally think that their own requirements are the most important. Different locations of the same organization, or different customers, want their own, idiosyncratic features, and it's no surprise that their demands do not take the overall business integrity of the product into account. That is the job of the analyst.

When piecemeal requirements arrive, the analyst needs to map them to the business processes that they affect. This mapping provides a way to show different people the effects (sometimes surprising) that a proposed change might have on their work. This analysis provides the analyst with the basis for discovering what people really need—and whether a change offers a real benefit or is just another feature tossed into the soup.

Another contributor to feature soup takes the form of designers including a new feature without considering its overall connections with the existing product. Designers should ask, "Is it within the declared scope?" "What are the interfaces with the existing product?" "Does it overlap or confuse anything that already exists?"

Repeated failure to address these issues leads to a product made up of disconnected fragments. The nature of requirements based on disconnected features means that there is no objective definition of what is in or out of scope. Hence, it is easy for extra requirements to seep into the project from a variety of sources—and they do. The more fragmentary the product becomes, the more difficult it is to assess and to make coherent changes; the downward spiral continues.

Organizations that stay out of the soup share a number of characteristics:

- Project goals and non-goals are defined as crisply and as early as possible.

- Project scope is declared and kept up-to-date against a precise definition of input and output data (see Pattern 24, "The White Line").
- Iron will is exercised in rejecting requirements that do not advance stated goals and fall demonstrably outside the project scope.
- New requirements follow an approved, traceable change-control process during which they are evaluated against the stated goals of the project.

Avoiding feature soup takes discipline. And it pays to keep in mind that it is you, the project team—not the requestors of piecemeal features—that will be in the soup.

53 Data Qualty

Data quality often sucks. A woefully common approach to this problem is to seek better software to process the data.

It's not unusual for the quality of database software to exceed the quality of the data it processes, yet from the end-user's viewpoint, system quality is limited by the lesser of the two. Companies everywhere are faced with databases full of inaccuracies and out-of-date or missing information. The problem is as obvious as the nose on your face, but like your own nose, it can be difficult to see. It's hard for companies to come directly to grips with their own data-quality problems, though nobody has trouble seeing the other guy's. What companies tend to see instead is a problem in the aggregate of software + data. Since the software is always easier to fix than the data (there is just so awfully much data), companies set out to fix or replace the software.

As none of this makes much sense, the essential thing to discuss here is not why we shouldn't do it, but why we do it even though we shouldn't. Part of the reason is a special instance of news improvement (see Pattern 45): The bad news that 2.4 percent of this month's invoices were returned as undeliverable makes its way up the hierarchy, being greeted at each level with the angry question, "Well, what the hell are *you* going to do about this and damn quick?"

The damn-quick part immediately precludes extensive manual fixing. The vague answer is that a serious "data cleansing" effort will be started pronto. This charming little phrase means different things as it moves up toward the CEO level. At the bottom of the hierarchy, data cleansing means getting on the phone and Internet and poring over correspondence files to research and correct each separate bad datum. At the top, it means working smarter, somehow teasing out the right data by cleverly processing the bad data. Since funding comes from the top, the funds that are allocated are typically tied to the working smarter approach rather than to a small army of clerks to do the real work.

It's worth pointing out that data can be corrupted (for example, by incorrect computing), and in this case, there are some at least partially automated ways to undo the damage by retrieving earlier backed-up versions. Similarly, when the same data are separately recorded in multiple systems, some automated data cleansing can help to isolate the better variant. In both cases, automated data cleansing depends on an ability to exploit data redundancy. While it's easy to imagine an example of redundancy coming to our rescue (System A has an old address, but here's a break: System B has the new one), real instances of poor data quality that can be automated away are few and far between.

The major cause of declining data quality over time is change. This spoilage in the asset we call "corporate data" can only be repaired by manual fix. Imagining otherwise just puts off the day of reckoning.

54 Ben

For some people, the work situation is so good, or the project is so interesting, or the product is so cool that they love their work more than they love their salary.

Ben—not his real name—works at a CAD software company. Ben is an engineer with an amazing grasp of higher mathematics. Apart from his normal project work, Ben helps people who have a problem they cannot solve unaided. (These are significant problems—Ben's coworkers are also very bright people.) Quite often, the problem is not within Ben's charter—sometimes not even within his division of the company—but he spends some time with his coworkers and they usually come up with a good solution.

The point of this story is that Ben takes great pleasure in his work. This is a man who does difficult things and succeeds. He loves his work, is challenged by it, thinks it is cool, and is definitely not there for the money. A pay raise or a bonus would obviously be welcome, but it would do nothing to motivate Ben. And while Ben feels more for his work than he does for his organization, he will not move to another for the sake of a pay raise alone.

We meet many Bens; we work with them from time to time in our consulting assignments. They work at many levels of their organizations, doing very different things. They are not always the most skilled people on the team, nor the highest paid. But you know when you meet Ben by the satisfied (but never smug) look on his face and the calm air of someone enjoying that day's work.

Although Ben is easy to manage (and it's a pleasure to do so), he is even easier to mismanage. One odious manager did not hire a replacement when one of his own workers left. Knowing how much Ben enjoyed his work, the manager thought he could shift more of it to him. The manager progressively loaded the work onto Ben, but as soon as the workload reached an intolerable level, Ben stopped enjoying the work and walked out. And because this was Ben, it was the best worker who was leaving.

The manager lost far more than Ben did. Bens always find work quickly, but it is difficult for a manager to find a Ben.

Bens don't need close supervision. The role of Ben's manager is to steer him gently toward the kinds of work that he finds interesting, thus assuring that those tasks will be accomplished with the fervor of a highly competent worker doing what he loves.

55 Miss Manners

It is considered impolite to question a fellow team member's idea.

There are organizations in which any kind of criticism is considered personal and therefore taboo. Somehow, the work product and the work producer are packaged as one. The odd logic goes like this: "A criticism of Meg's schema is a criticism of Meg's ability, and that is a criticism of Meg, the person. I won't criticize Meg, because that would hurt Meg's feelings and would open the door for others to criticize me for criticizing Meg."

It's not just straightforward criticism; it bleeds into any kind of implied criticism, such as a review or assessment. Any review short of "Great job, Hal" is socially uncomfortable for everyone in the room.

The result of this misdirected civility is deep mediocrity. Serious improvement is highly unlikely, and any kind of complete restart or rewrite is just about impossible. No one is ever going to say, "Let's trash this code and rethink the whole front end," even when it's the best thing to do.

The source of false good manners is a clear, but never publicly stated, message from somewhere on-high in the organization. It is a form of cowardice that is disguised as politeness.

"We will always try our best to be polite to one another" makes sense and is agreed to in most healthy organizations, but in a Miss Manners shop, this rule has a subtext. It is "We will not allow criticism, because once begun, it could spread, and our culture is not strong enough to benefit from such introspection. Decisions can't be proven best or worst, so accept all decisions without comment."

Miss Manners organizations are all facade and no face. People who populate them are obliged to wear masks all day long.

56 Undivided Attention

Full-time involvement in a single project improves individual performance.

When Derek Jacoby gave his wonderful performance as Alan Turing in the play *Breaking the Code,* in London's West End, he worked exclusively on that play for its entire run. Instead of accepting several roles in repertory, he devoted all of his attention and intelligence to that one play. He learned his lines, rehearsed with the other actors, investigated Turing's life, and determined how he could best portray the great mathematician, logician, and cryptographer. Then he performed the role every night.

The culture of the theater bestows success upon productions with actors such as Derek Jacoby, who devote themselves to one play at a time. We have found that software project cultures often succeed when developers make a similar investment in singular efforts.

Employers hire knowledge workers to take advantage of their ability and brainpower. Suppose you hire a specialist and he has a notional top brainpower production rate of 100 units per hour. As an employer, you want to do everything you can to make sure he operates at his top rate. You do the obvious things to take care of his creature comforts and to create an infrastructure with the tools and assistance necessary to maximize his focused time. Then you assign him to work full-time on a project, and he focuses his brain and works at maximum possible brainpower. Let's say that he works for 40 hours at top rate— he has given you 4,000 brainpower production units. You are doing everything you can to profit from the brain you have hired.

What you get from this transaction is *undivided attention,* the product of a positive connection between top brainpower production rate and dedicated work on one project.

Workers who are assigned to multiple, concurrent projects cannot maintain the top brainpower production rate because there is a price, in brainpower units, to pay for multitasking. Switching from the context of project A to project B requires some brainpower for understanding the project B status. Finding all the right project B files, clearing project A thoughts from the mind, reestablishing contact with project B people, and rehashing thoughts that were previously settled— these steps are all necessary for the brain to get reoriented into the context of project B.

> "By doing two things at once, you've cut your IQ in half, and believe me, those 40 points can really make a difference."
> —Dale Dauten, *The New York Times* (April 29, 2007).

In the best situation, the loss of productivity is minimized because your worker can call upon coherent and consistent documentation, to help speed up reorientation. But what about knowledge that isn't documented but is nevertheless clear to people working on the project? To be able to function effectively, the engineer needs to be conscious of previous discussions with customers and management, project meetings, outstanding issues, and many other aspects of the project history. In addition to the time needed to reconnect with the project's artifacts, there is a time cost in reestablishing personal relationships with other team members. Day-to-day contact between members of the team produces strands of experience that act as a jelling agent. Absent or unreachable team members water down the strength of that jell.

Some have attempted to quantify the cost of context-switching,[1] but the multitude of variables involved make estimation difficult. However, based on our observations of human concentration and information transfer, we are confident that context-switching causes a significant decrease in productivity. Organizations that recognize this connection between context-switching and productivity facilitate undivided attention by avoiding assigning an individual to multiple, parallel projects.

[1]Gerald Weinberg estimates that the context-switching cost of assigning three projects to one person is 40 percent. In other words, 40 percent of your worker's time is lost to nonproductive tasks. The other 60 percent is split among the three projects. In a 40-hour week, supposing equal time spent on each project, the worker ends up spending 8 hours on projects A, B, and C, respectively, and a massive 16 hours context-switching. The potential 4,000 brainpower production units is reduced to 2,400. See Gerald M. Weinberg, *Quality Software Management, Vol. 1: Systems Thinking* (New York: Dorset House Publishing, 1992).

57 "There's No Crying in Baseball!"

The organization's culture drives conflict underground by discouraging displays of emotion.

I once had an acquaintance from an ad agency remark to me, "It must be wonderful to work in software development where people never have occasion to get mad at each other."

—TDM

From the outside, the software industry must seem like a haven from emotional display; from the inside, it looks entirely different. Emotions are often high, and there is a lot of passion over matters that, except to insiders, wouldn't seem to justify any passion at all. In this respect, software is similar to many other kinds of knowledge work.

Most knowledge work is a relatively new phenomenon in companies that were once almost totally industrial. Think of AT&T, for example: A few decades ago, most of its workers were low-skilled and wore blue collars; today, it is all knowledge work. With such antecedents, it's easy to understand why many knowledge-work companies early adopted an unwritten rule that display of emotion would not be allowed in the workplace. This rule has been routinely violated, but it still persists. Someone who cries in a meeting or bursts out angrily, upon learning of an unwelcome decision, is written off as unprofessional. Such people are often thought too volatile for promotion. The net effect is to make passion and promotion mutually exclusive, hardly a recipe for success.

In deciding whether or not to tolerate unruly emotions, it's worth remembering that feelings intrude on work only to the extent that people care about their work. The easy way to make the feelings go away is to hire people who don't give a damn.

Staffing a project with people who care passionately about what they're doing *is* a recipe for success. Their passion may boil over from time to time, but mopping it up is just part of the price you need to pay to achieve ambitious goals.

In the 1992 film *A League of Their Own,* Tom Hanks plays the often-inebriated manager of a women's professional baseball team. While he is chewing out one of his players in front of her teammates, she begins to blubber. He screams at her, "Are you crying? There's no crying. There's no crying in baseball. There's no crying in baseball!"

58 Cool Hand Luke

"Confrontation 2" by Chaim Koppelman, used with permission

A legitimate conflict is interpreted as a "failure to communicate."

Just as it is an error to assume that knowledge work can have no emotional content, so it is an error to misattribute a colleague's upset. Misattribute is something we do all the time. The most common form of misattribution is to blame any failure to harmonize on poor communication. This is the ultimate scapegoat. Even the most un–self-critical organizations are willing to blame themselves for lousy communication skills. As consultants, we often find ourselves on the receiving end of this self-critique, paradoxically often delivered in the most elegant and lucid manner. People can be at their most communicative when reporting on what bad communicators they are.

In the Paul Newman film *Cool Hand Luke,* a prisoner faces a sadistic jail warden who precedes each punishment with the statement, "What we have here is a failure to communicate." In this case, as in many others, there is failure involved, but no lack of communication. What passed between the two parties in the film was the convict's indomitable will to resist and the warden's raw, red hatred. Each understood the other perfectly.

The next time you hear someone in your organization refer to a failure to communicate, look underneath for the subtitle. It's likely to read, "I understand you clearly, but I hate what you're saying." Calling this a communication failure turns everyone's attention away from the real cause—legitimate conflict—and focuses attention instead on a false cause. The result is a more-and-more elaborate effort to communicate a message that is being flat-out rejected.

The deep-seated cause here is a belief that conflict in a business setting is somehow unprofessional. The reasoning goes like this: "We're all working for the same organization, so how can there be conflict unless someone is not acting professionally?" This question only makes sense if you believe that all parties in an organization are perfectly aligned. Organizations are big, messy organisms that are shaped by evolution as much as design. They are full of conflict. Their charters (if anyone has bothered to specify them) entail values that are sometimes mutually exclusive. The organization may assert a determination to maximize both quality and productivity, but there are always trade-offs between the two. The various component organizations that make up the whole are sometimes pulling in different directions: Engineering and Marketing are often at loggerheads; Sales and Finance may be slightly out of sync; Human Resources and Corporate Communications may not sing in perfect harmony. Some people in the organization have a perspective that spans one-to-five years out, while others have a one-day to one-month perspective. There is legitimate conflict everywhere.

When conflict is considered natural and perfectly professional, the parties turn to proven conflict-resolution techniques instead of the false god of improved communication. The result may not be perfect, but it is always better.

59 Shipping On-Time, Every Time

The team always ships its releases on-time.

Now and then, you will hear a software manager boast, "My team *always* ships on-time." That's a pretty impressive statement. Assuming that the team has shipped multiple times and that the software it builds is non-trivial, shipping on the baselined, planned date, 100 percent of the time, is quite an accomplishment.

However, teams that *always* ship on-time sooner or later have to lower the quality bar in order to hit the ship date. We're not saying that they do so on every release. But a team that never compromises its ship quality criteria will eventually miss a ship date.

Navigating a development cycle requires constant rebalancing of priorities and reallocation of resources. In general, organizations have five main "levers" with which to steer the project:

1. People: Who is assigned to the project?
2. Technology: What processes, methods, and tools are available to your team?
3. Scope: What features are you building? What platforms are you supporting them on?

4. Calendar time: When do you intend to ship?
5. Ship quality criteria: What degrees of completeness, correctness, and robustness must the product exhibit before you ship it?

If you have formulated a rational plan, you have balanced these factors at the outset of the project. As you proceed, however, some things change, and you discover that other things were not what you thought they were. So, you adjust some combination of the five levers to keep your project on track to a successful outcome.

As we saw in Pattern 28, "Time Removes Cards from Your Hand," the closer you get to the ship date, the less useful some of your levers become. For example,

- "Adding manpower to a late software project makes it later."[1] Adding people consumes both the project's calendar time and the effort of people already on the project. Adding people late in the game is rarely going to help you hit a ship date. If anything, it may contribute to slippage.
- Changing methods or tools entails retraining, and it is unlikely to accelerate the first project on which the new processes or tools are used. The learning curve consumes time.
- De-scoping only really helps if the features being de-scoped have not yet been developed. There typically comes a time in the release cycle when the product is essentially feature-complete: Most of the feature code has been written and is now being stabilized. You may save some time by cutting a complete feature, thus saving QA time, but de-scoping loses its value toward the end of the cycle.

When you encounter problems late in the release cycle, you often find yourself with only two operable levers: calendar time and ship quality criteria. If you have managed well, the problems you find late in the project are not going to be mammoth ones, but they may still require course correction.

If you really are committed to shipping exactly on-time, every single time, you are left with only one correction available: relaxing your ship quality criteria.

---

[1]Frederick P. Brooks, Jr., *The Mythical Man-Month: Essays on Software Engineering* (Reading, Mass.: Addison-Wesley, 1975), p. 25.

60 Food++

The members of the project team regularly eat their meals together, and when possible, plan and prepare them as a team.

During production of the wonderful anime movie *Spirited Away*, the director realized that the film would miss its summer opening unless the animation team quickened its pace. The team decided its best way forward was to work longer hours.

One night, when everybody was working late, one of the team artists took it upon himself to cook *spaghetti all'amatriciana*. Everybody

who was still at work—and there were quite a few of them—ate together and declared that they loved the experience. The following night, a different team member decided she would cook for everybody, and the night after that, someone else took a turn cooking. And so, a team tradition came about.

Each night, one or other of the team members would prepare a meal for everybody. Even the director, Hayao Miyazaki, decided to show off his skills and cooked a noodle dish that was a culinary triumph. This simple act of cooking for the rest of the group had a galvanizing effect: The animation team met its deadline, and the movie opened on time.

The rituals surrounding food—the preparation, the interactions while eating, the cleaning-up process—forge a bond among all who participate.

One team we knew was obsessive about its food. At lunchtime, one or more of the team members would rearrange tables in the cafeteria—this was strictly against cafeteria policy—so that the entire team of sixteen could sit together. Places were guarded and interlopers were turned away until the entire team was seated and eating together.

These teammates didn't eat together because the project manager asked them to—they felt it was part of being a team, and they *wanted* to eat with each other.

When late nights were called for, to meet some pressing deadline, the members who were not needed for urgent work would drive to the supermarket and bring back food. They could just as well have gone home instead, but they stayed to provide food for the late workers and to eat with them.

You will notice that something almost magical happens to a team when it plans and prepares a meal. First, there is the adventure of gathering ingredients. This is not fast food, and some teams thrive on making the search difficult by demanding hard-to-find ingredients. Then comes the preparation: The skilled cooks do the difficult preparation, while kitchen slaves (as they are affectionately known) take care of the grunt work. Still others set the table, and so forth.

The food, when it arrives, is a team product. "We built this, we made it all come together, and now we are going to enjoy eating it" is the collective thought of the team as it sits down to the communal meal. And for teams working on long, amorphous projects, this is a "project within the project," one that can be completed quickly and savored.

You can also see an example of food bringing people together in the café society that has sprung up around the world. People regularly schedule business meetings in coffee shops. Laptops and papers compete with cappuccinos and croissants for table space. The feeling of intimacy brought about by sharing food—we consider coffee a food—makes the meeting more valuable. It is particularly telling that salesmen, trying to establish a strong connection with their prospects, make frequent use of cafés and food.

Eating together does not guarantee that your team will succeed, just as not eating together does not condemn your project to failure. However, we observe that many successful teams take advantage of the rich interactions that are part of preparing and eating food together.

61 Orphaned Deliverables

People develop project artifacts that no one values enough to pay for.

Every process improvement initiative in the systems and software industry defines a flood of new activities, roles, and artifacts. For example, the Rational Unified Process and the German V-Model suggest more than 150 deliverables, each. These deliverables include requirements specifications, design documents, specific models, user-interface concepts, test plans, estimates, . . . the list seems endless.

Photo © James Rye

One of the artifacts that is never questioned is the final deliverable: the product. But what are the merits of the others? Do we need them all? Is it worth spending time and effort producing them?

Sometimes, the team spends time producing artifacts that nobody cares about. It realizes the waste of time and effort, but the process demands that each deliverable be produced. In such cases, the question to ask is, Who is the sponsor of this artifact?

> spon•sor: *a person or organization that supports an activity by pledging money in advance*

Every artifact needs a sponsor who is willing to pay for it. Paying, in this context, means not only being empowered to ask for the production of this artifact but also being able to grant the resources to produce it.

If the deliverable in question is required inside the project, the decision is easy. It is up to the project manager to decide whether producing the artifact helps or hinders in achieving the project goals.

A more difficult case occurs when deliverables are needed or wanted by somebody outside the project team and producing those deliverables is considered an additional burden on the project. In such a case, a sponsor has to be identified.

Consider what happens when an organization wants all projects to come up with standard documentation of their software architecture. The hope is to foster reuse of design solutions and to inform outsiders about the project. The required architecture documentation includes attractive summaries of the most important decisions and overview presentations in a predefined format. However, the development teams' key goal is to finish on time and within budget. They do not need all this documentation to achieve their goal. A central architecture group could serve as a sponsor in this situation: It could lend a member at the start of the project to help the teams conform to company architecture standards and to help produce the required documents.

Maybe a sponsor in Marketing is needed to produce customer-specific user documentation in addition to the standard user manual. In order to get the required documentation done in time, he might contribute a marketing person to the team to take responsibility for producing these specific user guides during the current release.

Another sponsor could be the head of the central human-machine interface team who wants mock-ups for early feedback and has a manpower budget assigned for this job.

Other people from outside the project can act as sponsors, such as a central quality group that has a budget for collecting long-term statistics about post-release, error-removal rates. This sponsor offers manpower or time and money to the project to do this extra work, usually something that the project manager would be reluctant to fund from his own budget.

It is easy to ask for things to be produced when you do not carry the burden of justifying the costs. Most centralized methods and tools departments are not in a position to give resources to projects. Their job is to suggest what they think are good ideas and to persuade every project to go along with them. But since they are ministers without portfolio, their recommendations are not always welcomed by projects.

Orphaned deliverables are those produced without articulated and proven need; in other words, without a sponsor. Consider the merit of each orphan. If you find that nobody is willing to pay for it and that the project doesn't need it, don't do it. If you think it is a good idea but nobody is paying for it, find a sponsor.

62 Hidden Beauty

"Copenhagen Underground" by Michael Altschul

Some aspect of the project's work moves beyond adequate, beyond even elegant . . . and reaches for the sublime.

Some of us produce work that is intended for other eyes. If you're the body designer of a new car style, for example, then a large part of the success of your work depends on the extent to which it is appreciated by others. If what they see pleases them, you will know it and derive pleasure and esteem from their response. If you're good, this derived pleasure is a large part of your total remuneration package; depriving you of it would be like neglecting to pay your salary, practically a breach of your employment agreement.

Now imagine instead that you are designing the self-test mechanism for airbags on the same vehicle. Almost no one will see the result of your work or even be more than marginally aware that it is there at all. So, one might suppose that success or failure of this work—and any attendant satisfaction that brings—should depend entirely on whether or not it achieves its assigned functionality, with no provision at all for aesthetics.

What an error! Design is an inherently creative process in that it produces something where before there had been nothing at all. The act of creation can take you in many different directions, all perhaps functionally identical, but differing in ways that can only be termed aesthetic. Some designs are, quite simply, beautiful. Their beauty is not an added attribute, not a "decoration," but a side effect of achieving functionality in a way that is at once natural and yet surprising. This can be just as true of those parts of the whole that are largely or totally hidden as it is of those that are visible to all.

> *Since the inventor of Ethernet, Bob Metcalfe, is a friend, I thought I might look into the details of the Ethernet protocol to see how it was designed. I opened the spec to be informed, not charmed, but to my surprise, I found that the protocol was a thing of substantial beauty. It was spare where it needed to be spare, elegant in concept, and its recovery mechanism for lost packets was a simple derivative of the way the packets were originally transmitted. Its concept of collisions and the way it deals with them was unexpected, at least to me, but amazingly simple. Call me a weenie, but the Ethernet spec brought a lump to my throat.*
>
> —TDM

There is an aesthetic element to all design. The question is, Is this aesthetic element your friend or your enemy? If you're a manager, particularly a younger manager, you might be worried that any aesthetic component of the designer's work could be a waste, little more than the gold-plating that we're all taught must be avoided. This aesthetics-neutral posture in a manager acts to deprive designers of appreciation for work that is excellent, and to refuse acknowledgment of any valuation beyond "adequate."

The opposite posture requires that you be capable and willing to look in detail at your people's designs, and be aware enough to see quality when it's there. Doing this for even the shortest time will quickly convince you that the gold-plating argument is a red herring; no design is made better in any way by piling on added features or glitz. Rather, what enhances a design's aesthetic is *what is taken away*. The best designs are typically spare and precisely functional, easy to test and difficult to mess up when changes are required. Moreover, they make you feel that there could be no better way to achieve the product's assigned functionality.

When their work is largely invisible, designers are enormously affected by a manager who pores into the details enough to appreciate design quality. When you delve deeply into one of your designer's work, you may be able to increase the universe of people able to appreciate a lovely piece of work, from one to two. In the eyes of that worker, you just may be transformed from an okay manager to "the boss that I would follow anywhere."

"Perfection is reached not when there is nothing left to add, but when there is nothing left to take away."
　　　　　　　　　　　　　　　—Antoine de Saint-Exupéry

63 I Don't Know

The organization makes it safe to tell the truth even if that means not having an immediate answer.

You are at a meeting, and the project manager asks you whether all the data needed for the proposed marketing analysis is contained in the current database. You know quite a bit about the database and its contents, and you know it has most of the necessary data; but there are a few items you are unsure of, and these will be crucial to the marketing analysis.

In these circumstances, the truthful answer to the project manager is, "I don't know," but is it okay to say those words in your organization? Or are you obliged to dissemble and evade and do anything you can to avoid "I don't know"? On the other hand, if you do admit that you don't know, is this heard by your teammates as a sign of weakness?

In some organizations, the words "I don't know" are heard as "I don't yet have the answer, but I will." The words open the door to discussion and to exploring ways of finding the answer.

> "If you tell the truth, you don't have to remember anything."
>
> —Mark Twain

Suppose you answer the question with "I don't know yet, but if I spend a couple of hours with Giovanni—he worked on the original design—then I'm confident we will come up with the answer." At this point, Augusta chips in and says, "Hey, I did an analysis of that data for another project. I have my notes, and I think they might answer your question; they could save you quite a bit of time." Apart from being the truth, "I don't know" acts as a collaborative trigger and encourages everyone who knows anything about the problem on hand to offer helpful input. We are not talking about a permanent state of ignorance—it's a knowledge gap that is declared so that it can be plugged.

The opposite of this pattern happens when "I don't know" is definitely not welcome. This happens when people do not know the answer but don't feel safe enough to admit it. Either they are afraid of losing the respect of their colleagues, or they are afraid their boss will get the impression they cannot do their job. Moreover, "I don't know" can be seen as a threat to a manager: When he is desperately clinging to a schedule, he decidedly does not want unknowns to appear and threaten the schedule. The idea that there are significant unknowns in the development process is simply not palatable. Most of these organizations see the development process as if it were a factory assembly line. There are almost no unknowns on an assembly line: "When the car reaches you, bolt on a wing mirror of the same color. Then wait for the next car." When a development team member says, "I don't know," it is heard as "Stop the assembly line until I figure out which way the mirror faces." This organization would rather keep the assembly line going without necessary components than allow a momentary pause in production.

"I don't know" is viewed in some organizations as a sign of the speaker's gutlessness. The culture is that everyone is expected to know everything. However, we are well aware that we do not know everything and have not since we were teenagers. This blinkered attitude results in people being loath to ask for help, even when the need is apparent to them. The result is that things take longer. But if the development project misses its deadline, the organization would rather point to other factors—incompetent management, lack of personnel, or almost anything—than admit that its development process could contain unknowns.

Whenever you hear "I don't know," you hear a declaration of trust. If people feel safe saying "I don't know" throughout an organization, it indicates that people feel safe to ask for help. These are the organizations that truly encourage collaboration at all levels and reap the benefits.

64 Children of Lake Wobegon

The manager gives performance ratings that fail to differentiate sufficiently between strong and weak performers.

In *A Prairie Home Companion,* public radio fixture Garrison Keillor delivers the news from the fictional small town Lake Wobegon, "where all the women are strong, all the men are good-looking, and all the children are above average."

Performance ratings frequently fall into a narrow range suited only to the children of Lake Wobegon. Consider the example in Figure 64.1:

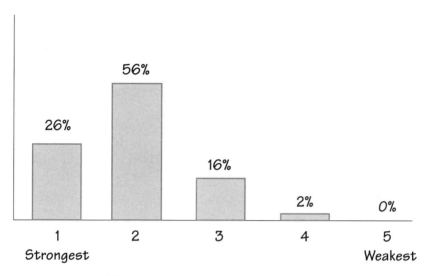

Figure 64.1.

This pattern is a symptom of management's failure to confront marginal performance and to recognize extraordinary performance. The "Lake Wobegon effect" is destructive for several reasons; first and foremost of these is that it reveals a culture of lying.

The one thing you can say with total confidence about the distribution of performance implied by the graph shown above is that it is not real. For how many decades have we seen consistent reports that individual performance in software engineering varies by an order of magnitude (or more) among the members of teams of any significant size? We accept these reported results in part because they conform to our own observations in the workplace. And yet, in far too many companies, the performance ratings turned in to HR once or twice a year tend to show relatively little variance from a near-universal "above-average" average.

The Lake Wobegon effect typically results from a combination of causes: HR-led confusion, senior management stupidity, and team leadership cowardice.

Human resources professionals create confusion when they issue contradictory guidelines for assessing and rating performance. A common example is mixing both *absolute* and *relative* criteria in the same performance-rating system. We have seen multiple examples of systems that in some places define the various levels of performance in absolute terms with respect to job requirements (for example, 1 = exceeds job requirements, 2 = consistently meets job requirements, 3 = usually meets job requirements, 4 = does not meet some job requirements, and so on). Elsewhere in the same system, a document specifies that the ratings are expected to conform to a preconceived distribution—say, 10 to 15 percent will be "1," 20 to 30 percent will be "2," 45 to 55 percent will be "3," and so on. These percentages imply that the ratings are relative to the employee population rather than to some absolute quality.

Senior managers sometimes create incentives to avoid confronting employees whose performance is deficient. One of the classics is this one-two punch:

1. "We're building a high-performing learning organization, so any employee who receives a performance rating of '4' or '5' must immediately be put on a performance improvement plan or 'managed out' of the organization."
2. "Due to a short-term budget squeeze, all open requisitions for new hires and replacements have been temporarily frozen until further notice."

In such circumstances, more than one manager has concluded (sometimes erroneously) that he will get more net work from a poorly performing Waldo than he would from an empty chair.

As much fun as it is to blame things on HR and bozoid executives, the most common reason managers don't confront marginal performance lies closer to home: It's difficult to get it right, and in any case, having a really frank discussion with a poor performer always feels terrible. So, managers put it off.

Constructively engaging with a poorly performing employee at some point requires the manager to shift roles slightly. During the early stages of performance management, the manager is in coach mode: explaining, demonstrating, assisting, answering questions, and above all, encouraging the employee. When it comes time to assess performance and to render some kind of rating, the manager has to act more as a judge. "Here is what you accomplished," he says. "These things went well; these others left room for improvement," and so on.

When the employee in question is not meeting the expectations of the role, this inadequacy is frequently not apparent to the employee *unless and until* the manager switches from coach to judge.

Since this switch is relatively infrequent (rarely more than four times per year, often fewer) and is almost always uncomfortable for both manager and employee, it is easy to see how the judge role's message can be muted or even omitted.

In addition to the Lake Wobegon effect, failing to confront marginal performance has another tell-tale symptom: the "shrink-wrapped job." As Waldo fails—and as you fail as his manager to confront his poor performance—you may instead take things off his plate, things you need to have done right. His more-capable peers (and you) pick up the slack. This happens gradually, but before too long, his apparent performance has improved to a tolerable level. Of course, this is only so because he's now doing far less than his role calls for.

What is so bad about using only a narrow portion of the performance-rating scale, and shrink-wrapping a few jobs? The simple answer is that it is unfair to your team members. You are lying to them about where they stand, and thus depriving them of the information they need to manage their careers.

You are lying to your very best performers by not letting them know that you know how really spectacular (and appreciated) their work has been. Let's face it: Everyone on the team knows who walks on water, including those doing so. Recognizing such contributions is the right thing to do. If that means giving an astronomical performance rating, then do it.

You are lying to your weaker performers by not giving them an early warning that their performance imperils their employment. Sometimes, poor performance results from failing to understand expectations, and sometimes employees can—and do—correct their performance. They go on to succeed or even excel if they learn early enough that they are not cutting it.

You are lying to many of those rated in the middle of the pack by implying that the middle is larger than it really is. An excellent performer who doesn't receive top ratings is not sufficiently recognized and rewarded. At the same time, a marginal performer receiving a "3" rating in a five-point system will feel more comfortable if 50 percent of all employees get "3" than he would if only 20 percent do.

You are telling the truth only to the truly average.

65 Co-Education

The project's stakeholders understand that each has much to learn from the others.

When a project is formed, its purpose is to change the state of some system, piece of work, product, or service. That much is obvious.

However, when a project starts, it is unrealistic to expect that any one person, or group of people, knows precisely what the desired future state is to be.

For example, it is unrealistic at the start of a project for builders to expect consumers to recite all of the requirements completely and accurately. Similarly, consumers can barely expect builders to understand the requirements before studying the situation. Without an understanding of the requirements, attempts at change are almost certain to founder.

The usual problem is that stakeholders don't understand that they have to learn from each other. What's required is a *co-education* effort between consumers and builders. Each must teach and learn from the other.

Let's look at this a little more closely. The requirements gatherers have to learn the consumers' work in order to specify an effective product or service. However, three obstacles may block the consumers from imparting their knowledge to the builders. First, the consumers may know their work so well that it seems obvious—they may fail to mention details they assume the builders already know. Second, the consumers are not necessarily equipped with great communication skills and may become reluctant to volunteer information that would otherwise help the builders. Third, the consumers may have difficulty identifying or envisioning their future needs. It is difficult, if not impossible, to know what we want until we see it.

Consider the experience of browsing in a bookstore and finding yourself interested in a book on a subject you've never considered before. Or if you don't often browse for books, imagine discovering an exciting item while shopping in your favorite category—maybe it's a snappy electronics gadget or a dreamy item of lingerie. (Readers will have to determine their own gender preferences for that last sentence.) Simply put, we most likely have to see or experience something before we can know whether it fits our needs and wants.

So, if builders must deliver to consumers a product or service that is as delightful as that book, gadget, or lingerie—without knowing in advance the qualities of that product or service—a two-way co-education must take place. Unfortunately, there are some obstacles that usually prevent meaningful learning from taking place between consumers and builders: the signed-off specification, the misguided solution, the learning lockout, and the absence of a common language. We discuss these below.

Some organizations insist that the requirements specification must be signed-off before any development can commence. This signing usually falls to the chief consumer. Since he will be held accountable for the specification, he naturally decides to dictate it. This reduces the role of the requirements gatherer to that of a stenographer, precluding the discovery and learning process that would be fostered by early prototypes and exploratory models.

Co-education may also get blocked by the proposal of a misguided solution. Some stakeholders take the stance that they know what they want, and, by George, they are going to get it. In such cases, what they want is some perceived solution to an immediate problem. However, that solution rarely addresses a multitude of larger needs: those of the work situation, of the organization that houses the work, and of the stakeholders outside the organization. In this case, it is the problem itself that everyone needs to understand—the solution will come in time.

Learning is best started early. As a project progresses, ideas harden, expectations become more firm, talked-about solutions become more anticipated, and it becomes progressively more difficult for both builder and consumer to break out and learn something new about their intended product or service. When this early opportunity is not taken, the traditional roles of requirements provider and requirements gatherer become entrenched, making it tougher, much tougher, for innovation to flourish.

Each of the stakeholders knows something—usually quite a lot—and typically each of them knows something different, so they have to teach each other. However, for parties from different backgrounds to co-educate each other effectively, they need a common language—a project Esperanto, if you will. Most often, a modeling language serves best. Co-education entails a certain amount of trial and error, and modeling is the ideal vehicle. People are less likely to argue vociferously for their pet features—and more likely to think about lessons learned—when they know that everyone regards the models under discussion as disposable artifacts of the learning process.

If the right products and services are to emerge from a development project, then the needs of the consumers—and the features to support those needs—must be well understood. This kind of understanding comes when consumers and developers learn the requirements from each other. The hardest part is realizing the need for a concerted co-education effort.

66
Seelenverwandtschaft[1]

The organization allows a particular team to shortcut even the most fundamental rules of its development process.

Here are some of the traits you first notice about this kind of team:

- They revile scheduled meetings, but they hold lots of small, ad-hoc meetings, of which nearly all are—or soon become—design sessions.
- They prefer white boards to other media for writing down ideas, designs, and to-do lists.
- They work from incomplete, high-level requirements statements. They often skip written design documents altogether, and they move on to coding very early in the development process.

[1]Ask a German.

- They throw away and rewrite lots of code. As soon as they have demonstrated a feature, they start to rework it.
- They do all of this very, very rapidly. Typical feature development times are one-to-three days. Extremely complex features might take ten days. Many tasks are completed and ready for testing in less than half a day.

This is not a common pattern, but it is so remarkable that it is worth noting. For lack of a better term, we call these "guerilla" teams. They are generally more common in the Agile community,[2] but some have evolved guerilla behaviors independent of a specific method.

When you come from a conventional software development background, there is something quite disturbing about guerilla teams. They seem almost reckless, but there is just no denying that they make real progress at an amazing pace. They can cause you to revisit your reasons for valuing many of the more formal elements of the software development process.

So many of the things we do in software are based on some basic beliefs, such as, "The cost of finding and correcting a problem escalates radically as you progress through the development cycle." Therefore, we want to get the requirements (and design) right, as early as possible, and to avoid rework in later phases. There is an even more fundamental assumption at work here: Construction and verification of working software is too expensive to be done many times over; you only get one or two shots per project. While this may be generally true, guerilla teams succeed because they operate outside this generalization. They develop and test code so quickly that they truly can afford to discard vast amounts of it in the course of discovering what it is they need to build.

So, what are guerilla teams good for? Well, version one of a new product for sure, and sometimes version two. These teams are at their best exploring a relatively new problem space and devising innovative solutions for it. Although they can produce very good, very durable code, guerilla teams are wired for innovation.

---

[2] A good survey of agile methods and their underlying principles can be found in Alistair Cockburn's *Agile Software Development: The Cooperative Game,* 2nd ed. (Boston: Addison-Wesley, 2006). Or use www.agile alliance.org as an entry point.

Guerilla teams are like power tools with no safety devices. They can be amazingly productive or amazingly destructive, depending on how well they are led and directed. They also have some inherent limitations.

Guerilla teams are organic. They cannot be created quickly, and they absolutely cannot be created by mandate. They typically form around one or two compelling leaders. They add members slowly (because their standards are very high) and they remain together only as long as the leader stays. They can be effective for years, but when the team begins to break up, it happens very quickly.

They are inevitably small and co-located. Guerilla teams do not work particularly well with other teams, especially distant ones. Their internal team cohesion is extraordinarily high. This model demands very loose external dependencies. Consequently, they do not grow by very much, they do not relocate, and they do not network harmoniously.

It is important to know when to stop using a guerilla team. Because developers like these thrive on breaking new ground, they typically begin to lose interest in a product or system once it has become established. Guerilla teams rarely stick around for version five of anything. Long before that, you might want to consider transitioning to a more conventional team structure. You will need to find fresh territory for your guerilla teams to conquer, or they will find it for themselves, somewhere else.

A final warning about guerilla teams: *Posers abound*. Since this model is extremely attractive to developers at all skill levels, many small teams believe themselves to be guerillas, but the real thing remains rare. Before you bet your project on such a team, you need to be sure that you are dealing with Che Guevara, not Che Leno.

67 Phillips Head

A demonstrably better idea is, surprisingly, not immediately accepted.

Imagine being the American inventor Henry F. Phillips, who in the early 1930s dreamed up the now ubiquitous Phillips head screw and screwdriver. His invention was demonstrably better than the clunky slotted screw convention that had preceded it. As you may be reminded when you still occasionally encounter the old slotted variety, the driver keeps slipping out of the slotted screw, causing you to interrupt your work to mutter colorful imprecations. The Phillips head screwdriver, on the other hand, is self-centering and stays in.

The new invention was hands down better, but infuriatingly, people kept on using slotted screws. Phillips must have been distraught. His better invention was simply ignored. It was eventually going to be accepted, but he didn't know that. From today's perspective, you'd like to be able to get an encouraging word back to him in 1930:

> "Hang in there, Henry," you'd tell him. "History is going to rule in your favor. There will come a day when it will be simply unthinkable for a new product to come out with slotted-head screws. The Phillips head will rule."
> "Yes, but when? When?"
> "Well, it may take a few years, but then—"
> "Years!!! You mean it may be 1935 or 1940 before people switch over to my invention?"
> "Actually, we were thinking more along the lines of 1985 or 1990."
> "Mrghhhh."

Newer and better is not enough to assure immediate acceptance. It takes time. Organizations resist change and/or defer change during an extended period of decision-making. But it can be frustrating to those who invent and espouse better ideas to see their proposals ignored, or worse still, considered to death. In the military, considering something to death is called the "slow roll." During our years of project work, we've seen that almost every good new idea that has come along has been slow-rolled, at least for a while. Even in a supposed fast-developing industry like software, for example, some of today's accepted best practices took as much as twenty years to become accepted.[1]

If you're presently frustrated that a demonstrably better way that you've been advocating has not been embraced, then please take heart from this: The great inventors of our past—people like Thomas Alva Edison and Werner von Siemens—are not remembered for a single invention. Rather it was their ability to come up with new ideas again and again that distinguished them. Someone who is pushing one idea is a promoter, while someone who's got a history of coming up with multiple good ideas is an innovator. The transition from promoter to innovator takes years and decades, but it's honest and involving work and it comes with a surprising extra benefit: People are a lot more inclined to accept the ideas offered by a proven innovator.

---

[1] For an explanation of the 20-year lag, see Samuel T. Redwine, Jr., and William E. Riddle, "Software Technology Maturation," *Proceedings of the 8th International Conference on Software Engineering* (New York: IEEE Computer Society Press, 1985), pp. 189-200.

68 Predicting Innovation

Photo by Gabriel Bulla

The team balances its need for innovation with its employer's need for predictability.

If the systems you build are at all interesting, then you know that innovation is part of every project. Innovation means that your team will be doing something it hasn't done before, and that the success of the effort depends upon your people solving problems in new and different ways. At the same time, you are nearly always required to predict, with a reasonable level of accuracy, when you will be finished. This puts you in the business of predicting the arrival of good ideas, and that is not easy.

You probably understand this puzzle all too well: You need to walk a narrow path that provides your developers with enough time to explore, discover, learn, and solve, while at the same time providing your employer and customers with reasonably accurate expectations for the completion of the development effort. It's so easy to wander off this narrow path to one side or the other. If you set expectations too optimistically, you may very well pressure your developers to finish, and so limit their ability to get the right product. On the other hand, if you refuse to predict completion until very late in the development cycle, you may find your boss less than thrilled with your own performance.

The development planning process goes something like this: Even after you have a reasonable set of product feature requirements, you know that your developers may need several iterations before they can figure out what they need to build and how to build it. So you plan two or three early time-boxed iterations for prototyping and exploration. How long each iteration lasts depends on the nature and scale of the effort, but we typically see them lasting from one to four weeks each.

After two or three such iterations, most of the technical unknowns have become knowns, and development of final-state product features can begin. Here, too, iteration is important. Teams typically use anywhere from three to five additional iterations to complete the release. Once again, the duration of each iteration varies from team to team, but they often range from four to twelve weeks each. So, the overall development timeline for the release looks something like this:

Product Requirements Definition						
Itn 1	Itn 2	Itn 3	Itn 4	Itn 5	Itn 6	Stabilization

In this example, the first three iterations are focused on exploration and prototyping of the entire feature space. This does not mean that the result of Itn 1 will be a prototype of all the features that will be in the shipping product. It just means that the developers will be free to work on any aspects of the product that they choose. It also means that the result of Itn 1 may be completely discarded at the start of Itn 2. It is more likely that some of the Itn 1 code will form the basis of the Itn 2 work, but that is not a necessity. The goal of Itn 1 (and of Itn 2, and if necessary, Itn 3) is to work out the unknowns and to reduce the remaining uncertainty in the development effort. Altogether, Itn 1 through Itn 3 might take anywhere from six to twelve weeks. Your mileage may vary.

The final iterations (there may be three or two or six of these, depending on your situation) constitute the construction of the shipping product, most probably using some of the code developed in the first three iterations. These iterations typically take more time than the exploratory ones; they are usually four-to-twelve weeks long, depending primarily on the development method used by the team.

How does this approach help you balance innovation with prediction? Balance comes from building into a fixed development period multiple passes through those areas of the problem space that require innovation. Does this guarantee that your team will generate the required good ideas, at the right time? Of course not. But this approach allows several creative iterations to be planned as part of the overall development time frame.

Projects thrive on innovation; they also need predictability. However, too much or too little of either can be crippling.

69 Marilyn Munster

In some organizations, developers are kings; in others, they are pawns.

The Munsters was a situation comedy television show in the U.S. that began in 1964 and ran for two seasons. The shtick was the uproarious daily life of a family of monsters living in some regular town, at 1313 Mockingbird Lane. The dad, Herman Munster, is a goofy version of Frankenstein's monster; his wife is a vampire; Grandpa resembles Count Dracula via vaudeville; the son, Eddie, is a young werewolf.

Paradoxically, the Munster's live-in niece, Marilyn, is a beautiful blonde college student. But the rest of the family doesn't see Marilyn as beautiful. They see her as completely unattractive. They try to protect her feelings, but they're actually a little embarrassed by her. One of the central conceits of *The Munsters* is that Marilyn's low status is an accident of having been born into this strange family. It is clear that Marilyn would be far more appreciated in any other family in the neighborhood.

Many developers live the life of Marilyn Munster. They work for companies that rely on technology, but their work is largely unappreciated, and they have very low status in the organization. In many such organizations, managers have all the status. The manager holds the responsibility for planning, scheduling, tracking, estimating, and assigning work to technical staff. Planning, scheduling, tracking, and estimating are usually done exclusively by managers with other managers. The developer is a tech weenie, someone who "does not understand" the real hard work of managing the company.

Managers make the big money because they are responsible for choosing which projects to run, and for running those projects as chosen corporate investments. Techies are to put their heads down and build what the managers tell them to build. If they don't like it, they are free to leave; the managers, along with HR, will find a replacement. The replacement may be a contractor, and the contractor may be on another continent where tech weenies are less costly than at corporate HQ.

There is another variant of this pattern in which Sales has all the clout. After all, the reasoning goes, it doesn't matter how good your products are if they don't get sold to customers. The underlying belief in both these companies is that developers are abundant and that one is about as good as another, so they should be paid as little as possible for their services.

There are, of course, companies that take a completely different view of developers. These companies believe that their products and services are differentiated from their competition by quality and innovation. They realize that there is a massive difference in talent and productivity between the top 10 percent of developers and the average developer. They want the best they can get. This results in a culture in which the developer is king, having great latitude over his workload and his approach to accomplishing that work. These developers often define features as well as build them, and they are typically the front-line estimators of development work. Very senior developers can earn as much as team leaders, sometimes more. Most often, but not always, developers are kings in organizations that make software as their product or ship software as a principal component of their product.

There is an extreme developer-as-king culture that is dysfunctional. When the developers optimize their own work and schedule without regard to the impact of their decisions on others, projects can get into trouble. For example, we found a project where the two developers decided that they would frame-up the software—leaving many classes incomplete because they knew they could write them later—and worked only on "the interesting, hard bits." The rest of the project team, the QA folks, and the tech writers ended up facing a huge spike of work as the deadline loomed, because nothing was done. Nothing was testable and nothing could be documented until suddenly *everything* was done, once the developers filled in the gaps they had left. The developers had de-optimized the project by optimizing their own work.

If you employ developers, it is worth asking yourself how important quality and innovation are to the success of your organization. At the highest levels, quality and innovation both require truly talented developers. You won't attract, cultivate, and retain top talent if you treat them as a regrettably necessary cost center to be minimized.

If you are a great developer and are feeling a bit like Marilyn Munster, rest assured that there are other families out there who will show you the appreciation you deserve. Flee the freak show.

Interlude:
The Cutting Room Floor

Some patterns didn't quite make it into the book:

- When Your Manager Is a Midget
- If I Had a Hammer
- The ISO-Standard Condom
- Whistle While You Work
- The Corporate Charity: Skipping Against Halitosis
- The Ouija vs. Function Points: An Empirical Study
- You Be the Judge: Are They User Reps or Potential Organ Donors?
- If Your Name Really Is Dilbert . . .
- Cubicles Without Exits
- I Don't Usually Do Things Like This on the First Release
- Why St. Jude Is the Patron Saint for Testers
- No Dickheads or All Dickheads?
- A Mullet and Two Gold Chains
- Maori War-Chanting: The Next Team-Building Exercise
- Why the Cleaning Lady Was the Only Person Who Actually Read Your Entire Test Plan

- Save Valuable Time: Write Requirements After Beta
- Faith-Based Software Engineering
- Cheese Never Sleeps
- Rapture of the Bits
- Arriving in Bangalore After Midnight
- The Bedpan at the End of the Rainbow
- Requirements-Free Software Engineering
- HR Hires Our Astro-Physicists
- The Bozone Layer

70 Brownie in Motion

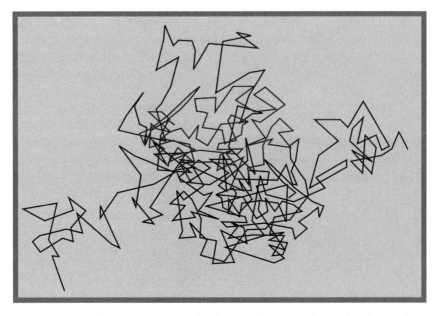

Team members are added to the project before its vision is properly formed.

In the early days of a new project, its leaders are under pressure to accomplish two things: define what the project will deliver, and make visible progress quickly.

The urge to gain momentum leads many managers to equate population with progress. They begin staffing the team before it is really clear what the new members should be doing. Naturally enough, the new recruits are largely uncoordinated. The result of having too many people with too little direction is random activity, or movement in haphazard directions, rather like the movement of pollen grains in water so famously observed by Robert Brown.

The opposite of this pattern is a project that develops a clear and coherent vision of what is to be done, while the staff remains limited to the essential few. The envisioners isolate themselves until they have developed the project's goals, its scope, its constraints, and a clear notion of the product to be delivered and what benefit that product shall bring to its intended audience or owners. This vision is complete—demonstrably complete—before additional team members are brought onto the project.

> *"Send 'em to the movies. At least until a core group has planned out the structure of the project, and defined what newly hired staff ought to be doing."*
>   —Steve Mellor

Two of your authors were involved in a long-term project at a major utility company to design and build its largest application system. The effort ultimately required several hundred man-years, but the basic concepts and high-level architecture were conceived by a team of only three people, over a period of three months. Similar cases abound: Today there are thousands of programmers around the world working on Linux, yet the vision for Linux came from only one person. The visioning of C++ was a one-man effort. On the other hand, a committee envisioned Ada.

Adding people to the project before the vision becomes clear is counterproductive. When too many people are trying to set the plans for the project, the result will be muddied and incoherent. Clear vision comes from an individual or a very small group, no matter how many people eventually form the team.

71 Loud and Clear

The project's goals are clearly and repeatedly articulated.

The goals of a project are its requirements and constraints at the highest level. These goals need to be stated early and revisited constantly by everyone on the project. Why? Because people working in an organization often have conflicting individual goals. The salesman wants to maximize the gross revenue from his sales, since his commissions are based on revenue. The product manager wants to maximize the profitability of his line, so his boss will consider him successful. The engineer wants to get all the promised functionality into the next release because a bonus is riding on it. These goals do not align; they may even be in conflict. Organizations are big, messy things, and unless conflicts are made visible, they will not be addressed.

A project can't be messy for too long or it will be rudderless. Up front, the goals need to be articulated, reviewed, and refined, so that there is a reasonable assurance that the various patrons and stakeholders have truly converged on an agreement for the expectations for the project. When a project is building a single system that straddles several city-states of organizational power, it may be no mean feat to find a single set of goals in a diverse community.

If the stakeholders can indeed find a set of nonconflicting goals, then these goals become the vision for the design and construction.

However, even if the goals have been properly defined, they are of little use unless they remain visible. Without constant reminding of the overall target for the project, it is too easy for people to forget them and lose sight of the project's main purpose.

Carolina, a business analyst with one of our clients, started a big project by getting the stakeholders together and helping them to converge on a common set of project goals. Then she wrote the resulting goal statements and their measurements in large letters on a poster-sized card (see Figure 71.1). She took this with her to all the project meetings and sat it on its own chair. Whenever things went off track, she used the goal to help people refocus: "Either the goal is wrong and needs to be revisited or we are going off track."

She says that two key factors contributed to the success of her approach: Everyone was heard when the goal was set, and the goal was kept visible to everyone throughout the project.

—SQR

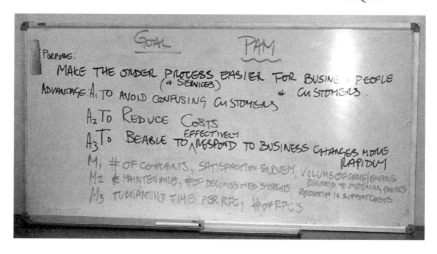

Figure 71.1. A Project's Purpose, Advantage, Measurement (PAM) Statement

Analysts and business people aren't the only ones who need to keep track of the goals. Designers need to know the goals in order to make informed design choices, asking for example, "What is the expectation for the operational life of the system? If we run it three times over its life, we may want to design differently than if it will run all day, every business day, for at least the next decade."

Just about every project is under time pressure, and as the project proceeds, it may become evident that not all features can make the first release. Which features make it into Release 1 is clearly based on decisions made by product and project management, and those decisions are anchored by the goals.

Having correct goals is crucial. Keeping everybody aware of these goals makes an enormous difference to the project and to the product it produces. Like Carolina, you need to give your goals a seat at the table.

72 Safety Valve

To counter the intensity of its work, the team devises a pressure-release activity that becomes a regular part of team life.

Nobody works a complete day—we can't. We like doing our work, but we all need to stop periodically to refresh ourselves, by doing something other than work. We are by no means slacking off when we get up and go down the hall for coffee—like a boxer between rounds, we need to take a break.

But there is another kind of break we need that is not to do with tiredness or refreshment. It is the relief we need from the pressure of our work. Most people engaged in projects work hard, and sometimes long, and often under the pressure of a tight deadline. This is normal; we would not want it any other way. However, from time to time, teams need a release from some of that pressure.

The mechanical safety valve pictured at the start of this piece releases steam when the pressure in a boiler climbs too high. Many project teams create their own safety valve, usually an idiosyncratic activity that becomes their special way of letting off steam.

Safety valves take many forms. Some are simple: For example, one team we know engages in spontaneous Silly String battles. Another team organizes races among the office cubicles, on miniature tricycles.

Other valves are more elaborate. One large team regularly plays a game called "Secret Assassin." Each team member is assigned a target and simultaneously becomes another member's target. Once these secret assignments have been made, team members stalk their target with a Nerf gun. They go about their work as they normally would, while hoping to catch their target before getting Nerfed by their own secret assassin.

Rather than take people away from their work, the game seems to do the opposite. One director of this company finds that productivity rises when a game of Secret Assassin is being played. The rules of the game may support this effect; for example, employees may not be assassinated at their desks.

At another company, on the first Friday of each month, the whole software development team heads off to a newly opened movie chosen by an e-mail poll. The surprising thing is not that people go to the movies, but that *everybody* on the team attends, regardless of the film being shown, and (almost) regardless of the project's demands.

Betting pools also serve as safety valves. One team conducts a sweepstakes on the daily pickup time of the UPS van, to the nearest minute. The typical kitty is barely enough to buy lunch, but the suspense always succeeds in breaking the tension of the team's work.

Safety valves like these are born within the team. Someone starts the activity, and it catches on with the rest of the team members. This kind of activity cannot be mandated or even suggested by someone outside the team. We have observed notable failures when management attempts to manufacture a safety valve for a team.

At one company, the HR department built a recreation area for developers—but nobody used it. An insurance company set aside a room, furnished it with couches and cushions, and posted a sign urging employees to use the room when they needed to relax. Again, nobody used it, preferring instead to stop by the large fish tank and watch the carp for a few minutes.

This is not to say that management or HR is incapable of facilitating a team's chosen release activity. Pool tables, ping-pong tables, dartboards, and similar diversions have all proved popular at various installations. However, the most effective and popular safety valves originate inside the team.

If you are a manager and see a team spending a little time on a safety-valve activity, please don't discourage it. And don't encourage it, either, for that is the team's playtime, and they know best how to use it.

73 Babel

The project fails to develop a consistent language that's understood by all members of the development team and stakeholder community.

We expect to be understood—and most of the time, that's a pretty safe assumption. When the people we are talking to share our contextual and cultural space, our meaning is usually communicated without distortion. In an English pub, when you ask for a pint, you get a pint of ale. Ask the driver of an electric dairy car in London for the same thing, and you'll get a bottle of milk. Similarly, when you are talking to a co-located fellow team member about the network status or the customer discount rate or any other term you use in your project, you expect to have a shared understanding of the meaning.

It is this optimistic expectation of being understood that prevents you from asking, "Does he really mean the same thing I do? Are we simultaneously nodding yet speaking different languages?"

Babel is encouraged by the fiction that organizations have a common language and that as long as every project uses this language, all will be well. But organizations are large, dynamic, inconsistent creatures, and terms like *service, order, asset, policy, customer, employee,* and *discount* have very different meanings, depending on their context of use within a project. Rather than rely on the wishy-washy generalities of org-speak, every project needs to define its own common language. The degree of formality and rigor required depends on the likelihood and seriousness of the risk of being misunderstood, with loss of human life at one end of the scale and minor financial loss or irritation at the other.

The risk is increased by any of the factors relating to differences between individuals, such as domain knowledge, life experience, linguistic background, or personality traits. The list becomes longer when you consider other influences, such as geographical separation, assignment to parallel projects, and outsourcing to other organizations. Many organizations grow through acquisitions, and each acquired company has its own idiosyncratic language that may have to be decoded and normalized by the new parent company.

The language you need for your project is a living language that truly reflects what all the team members are learning about the problem space. Cultivating the language means progressively defining your terminology in writing, to reflect your growing understanding. This also means making those terms easily accessible and extendable by everyone on the team.

When a team does develop a consistent language, the effort may be almost invisible from the outside. But inside the project, the participants are willing to focus attentively and repeatedly—almost obsessively—on definitions. The successful team is the one that does not accept the fiction that there is already an organizational common language. It is willing to refine and refine again in order to build its language, the one that will protect the project from Babel.

74 Surprise!

The manager offering rewards and incentives gets responses in addition to those he planned.

After six weeks of six- and seven-day workweeks, the release finally went in. The team was burned-out, but everyone on it was elated that the job was done and the system was on the air. After a brief hibernation from exhaustion, the team was back in the office, gathered around the project manager, who proclaimed victory and offered

heartfelt thanks on behalf of the company. To show its appreciation, the company gave each member of the team a voucher for dinner for two at one of the best restaurants in town. As the vouchers in envelopes were passed around, jokes about ordering jeroboams of Veuve Clicquot champagne, chateaubriand, and the entire dessert tray filled the conversation. Once the team broke up and most people had headed back to work, one team member approached the PM and said, "Have this voucher back. If my wife ever thought that I worked the last month-and-a-half, leaving her alone with our two kids, for one measly dinner out, she'd shoot me." The PM didn't know how to respond.

The voucher was not a bad idea. For all but one member of the team, it was seen as just a token. It said, "Go relax and splurge a bit on us." But one team member could not accept it as that. It would only look to his spouse as a cheap attempt at a buyout—no compensation for a huge amount of work that impinged on precious family time.

Rewards given from the organization to a team or to individuals are almost impossible to pull off perfectly, even when they are truly tokens, just thank-you gifts.

When organizations get in the habit of using prizes and rewards to entice a change in behavior or to sustain an unsustainable behavior, such as working six-day workweeks, they only succeed in antagonizing and demoralizing most recipients. Reward-giving organizations believe that they are positively reinforcing and recognizing outstanding performance, but they get caught up in a dysfunctional reward pattern in two ways: First, they give out rewards to the few, immediately spurring an unspoken emotional reaction of estrangement and inequity in all of the non-recipients: "How about me? I've been working my heart out over here. Where's my prize?"

Second, the prize, something that is supposed to be a pleasant surprise, turns into an entitlement. Past recipients develop expectations, wondering, "What do you think we'll get for finishing our project?" The prize has no positive effect at all.

Organizations that are locked into a pattern of rewards and prizes are never rewarded.

75 Fridge Door

Team members routinely display their work products for all to see.

You often hear about the "need to know" principle from managers: Pass to other people only what they need to know to perform their jobs; do not communicate information unless it is absolutely necessary for the task at hand; restrict the information flow to the bare necessity.

The Fridge Door pattern defies this advice, and yet correlates strongly to successful projects. Here's how it works:

Even though it is not vital for everybody to know everything, the team displays significant information in a highly visible form. It's in 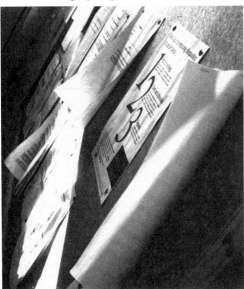 places where everybody on the project team is sure to look—when entering or exiting from the office or the project war room, or on the way to the coffee machine or the rest rooms. Some of the information can be updated—by almost anybody—in a casual way, with pencils and colored markers left for that purpose. These displays are living documents that contain important status and structure information.

Healthy teams share artifacts such as the following, from different roles in the project:

- a release plan
- work assignments for the week or for the current release, so everybody can see who is on what task during a particular period of time
- burn-down charts or any other form of progress report in an easy-to-grasp representation

The following requirements artifacts are often shared:

- the context diagram of the system, so everybody can see what belongs in the system, what is outside, and where the interfaces are.
- the list of use cases (or the use-case diagram), most often a one-page overview of the processes to be supported by the system. We often see it color-coded by stage of development of the process; for example, red for "planned," yellow for "under construction," and green for "done."
- a matrix of use cases versus domain classes (a sort of high-level cross-reference list matching domain entities to use cases).

Software architects often display the top-level structure of the software system—for example, the twenty most important components and their relationships. This is not to be confused with the slick presentation slides created for marketing purposes. It's the real structure that architects are working with, and you'll see a few hand-drawn corrections about new dependencies and some red question marks about unwanted dependencies.

Testers often proudly present overviews of their test cases and the coverage they are achieving with them. Even someone who is not part of the QA sub-team can get a pretty good understanding of how his work is affected by QA and testing.

Visual displays like these offer all project members an editorial opportunity to present what they care about and what they want others to care about, too.

> "With information radiators, the passersby don't need to ask questions; the information simply hits them as they pass."
> —Alistair Cockburn, *Agile Software Development*
> (Reading, Mass.: Addison-Wesley, 2002), p. 84.

A public display of project artifacts indicates trust among the team members; it sends the message that nothing is hidden for merely arbitrary reasons. There is no fear of having others detect incompleteness or schedule slips. Team members on fridge-door projects are substantially less inclined to "spin" or sugarcoat their progress reports.

The fridge door also saves on ponderous version management and document distribution. Many of these displays are updated on the fly and thus give up-to-date status information to everybody.

Walking down a corridor, you may see "We just improved the name of the interface to the accounting system, to better reflect the fact that it is not discrete but an online stream of information." Around a corner, you may see another posting: "Did you see that the latest requirements change has thrown us back by 4 days compared to yesterday's sprint plan?"

There is something very natural about fridge-door displays. Shared artifacts not only demonstrate pride in achievement, but also provide the "you are here" function for projects, literally keeping everyone on the same page. Compare this to a culture that sports motivational posters adorned with mountain climbers, rowing teams, galloping white horses, and a tired variety of feel-good phrases.

Where would you prefer to work?

76 The Sun'll Come Out Tomorrow

The manager believes that average future progress will exceed average past progress.

You manage several project teams. You have just poured yourself a cup of coffee and are settling into a conference room with your team leaders, about to review the progress of some of your current development efforts. The first project on the agenda is new to you. It has been under way for

a couple of months, but came under your leadership only recently, due to a reorganization. The project manager is relatively junior, but you have heard great things about him. Let's call him Jerry.

Jerry begins by bringing you up to speed on the project. He is using three-week iterations, and his team has just completed the third of them. During each of the first two iterations, the team did not get through all of its planned work, and had

to carry some of it over into the subsequent iteration. The trend continues. At the end of three iterations, the team has completed only what it had planned to finish in the first two. (Some of the specific work elements have changed, due to shifting priorities and a little bit of scope creep.)

You're not exactly delighted to hear all of this, but at the same time, it's not entirely surprising. Eager teams tend to be a bit too optimistic about the amount of ground they can cover, especially early in the development cycle. So, it shouldn't be too difficult to make some course corrections. After all, there are five more development iterations before the planned beta release, with four additional iterations planned for stabilization and for responding to customer feedback on the beta. You just want to ensure that Jerry is thinking about how he will close on these milestones, so you ask, "What adjustments do you have in mind, given the progress thus far?"

Jerry: "Actually, we're pretty confident that we can stick to the original scope and schedule."

You: "But in order to do that, you would have to complete six iterations' worth of work in the next five iterations."

Jerry: "Yes, and we think that's entirely reasonable. We've got a great team, and everyone is stoked to make these dates."

You: "That's great to hear, but then how do you account for the slippage you've had during the first three iterations?"

Jerry: "Oh, that. Well, it was no single big issue; it was a bunch of little things, strictly one-time type setbacks."

You: "Tell me about a few of them."

Jerry: "Sure. Well, there was that big network outage last month. The outage itself lasted only eighteen hours, but recovering from it cost us a couple of days. Then Darlene's father died suddenly, and she was out for a week. As you know, she's our product manager, so we are dependent on her both for requirements and for acceptance of completed features. Then Sales popped up two weeks ago, needing help with a proof of concept for this massive deal they're trying to close. That one took three guys off-line for several days."

You: "You're right. That's pretty unusual. Anything else?"

Jerry: "Just a couple of others. You know about the big day-light-saving time fiasco? Well, that caused a bunch of customer support cases that required time from our developers. And, oh yeah, Jason got called up for jury duty, and since he had postponed it three times, this time they made him do it. He was out for two weeks, and he was the key dev. on the off-line support feature. So, we had to push that off until later."

You:	"Wow. One thing after another. Given all that, you and your team did a great job getting as far as you did through three iterations."
Jerry:	"Thanks. Like I said, they're a fantastic team."
You:	"So, what percentage of your time during iterations four through eight have you set aside for problems like these?"

[Uncomfortable silence.]

Jerry:	"Well, uh, we don't anticipate having any more problems like these. These were exceptions. You can't know when things like these are going to happen. I mean, the whole daylight-saving time problem was caused—literally—by an act of Congress. How often is that going to happen?"
You:	"So, let me make sure I understand. You figure that you can hit the original dates without having to cut any features, because you have incurred all your bad luck during the first three iterations, and from now on, all your luck will be good?"

Jerry is not a bad manager. Jerry is a dangerously optimistic manager. This may be because he holds an optimistic view of the world and cannot believe that some number of as-yet-unpredictable setbacks will befall his project in the future. But even if Jerry is not a natural optimist, the dynamics of the project may give him an incentive to behave like one.

Consider Jerry's more realistic alternatives. If he assumes that his project will experience *average bad luck* in the future, he will most likely have to consider some combination of scope reduction and schedule extension. (Yes, he could seek additional resources, but this is less likely to aid his project in the short term.) Depending on how Jerry perceives that *you*—his manager—would react, Jerry may be unwilling to declare the need to make such painful changes.

Jerry's reluctance to propose feature cuts, or a new ship date, may also arise from the fact that—at this point—he can't *prove* that he needs them. The planned work fits, if only barely, into the time remaining, if and only if nothing goes wrong. If Jerry did ask to cut a feature to make allowance for future bad luck, and you or someone else challenged the need to do so, Jerry couldn't point to any one specific problem that justifies the cut, because it hasn't happened yet.

Extreme Programming offers an elegant approach to counter-acting this kind of optimism; it is called "yesterday's weather."[1] The productivity of the next iteration (the one being planned) is assumed to be no greater than the actual productivity experienced on the prior iteration (the one just completed). Whether you use yesterday's weather or your own adjustment, the one thing you know for sure is that your project's future bad luck will not be zero. So, plan accordingly.

---

[1]Kent Beck and Martin Fowler, *Planning Extreme Programming* (Boston: Addison-Wesley, 2001), Chapter 8, pp. 33–34.

77 Piling On

Stakeholders profess support for a project but then keep adding bloat until the project founders.

"Piling on" in American football is a penalty called when defensive players leap onto an already downed ballcarrier. The weight of massive linemen landing on the ballcarrier's back is intended to send him a message, just in case he might ever again have the temerity to carry the ball into their territory. It is justly called a foul.

Piling on in project work usually takes the form of adding marginal features to a product whose cost/benefit ratio hangs in the balance. While seeming to be constructive, the covert goal of such behavior is to add dead weight. This is a variation on what author Peter Keen calls "counter-implementation." In his classic paper,[1] Keen offers the intriguing observation that those who would defeat a new project have no need to take the risky step of actually coming out against it. Rather, they can give it the ultimate vote of confidence by suggesting a few dozen additions and improvements that will "help the project achieve its extraordinary promise."

[1] Peter G.W. Keen, "Information Systems and Organizational Change," *Communications of the ACM,* Vol. 24, No. 1 (January 1981), pp. 24–33.

Project teams that practice a lot of iteration are not immune to piling on, but they do have a natural and powerful defense against it: As they plan the sequence of iterations, they are obliged to assess features from the essential to the piled on and to allocate priorities accordingly. The early implementations have the essential features and the others are added to the tail end. When adding the next feature promises an incremental benefit that's less than its incremental cost, the project may well be declared finished. Since all the meat has been delivered early, the impetus to keep the project going is negligible.

Counter-implementation in all of its forms (you really need to read Keen's paper) is so common that if you don't see it, you're not looking hard enough.

78 Seasons for Change

Windows of opportunity for scope changes are opened at specific times throughout the project, typically aligned with the boundaries of development iterations.

Software development projects present us with a stream of choices to make. Some choices are fundamental, while others have only a limited effect. Of the former, one of the most influential decisions we make during development defines the scope: What is in and what is not.

Woodcut by Bobby Donovan

The determination of a project's scope has a catch–22 characteristic: You need to get it right as early as possible, but you almost always need to adjust it as you go. Ultimately, since you want to complete the work, your tolerance for scope changes must gradually diminish, as depicted in Figure 78.1.

If you interpret this picture literally, you may infer that scope changes happen continuously, throughout the project. While that *could* happen, most project managers realize that it's impractical to entertain every scope change as it arises. Why? Because scope changes are disruptive. They can have a profound effect on what people do day-to-day. People reassess what they're doing, in light of the change, and that slows down the project.

To balance the need to refine the scope with the need to maintain forward momentum, many teams divide development projects into

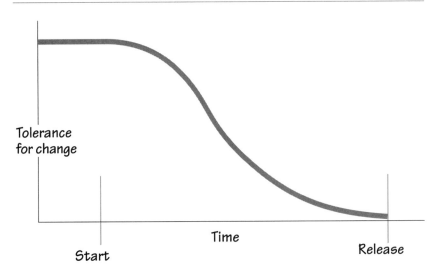

Figure 78.1.

short iterations, each with restrictions on scope changes. The initial
scope definition is used for the first iteration, and it cannot be changed
until the iteration is complete. Meanwhile, those planning the second
iteration may consider scope changes. But during each iteration, developers and others on the team are not disrupted.

The pattern looks something like Figure 78.2.

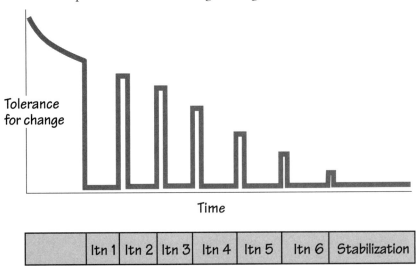

Figure 78.2.

It's worth mentioning that this approach only works well if iterations are kept relatively short. Deferring all scope changes during longer iterations—say, twelve weeks long—is not always wise, and sometimes not even possible. Iterations of two-to-six weeks seem to minimize disruptions from scope changes without stifling the evolution of the project itself.

79 Paper Mill

The organization measures progress by the weight and number of documents produced to date.

A project is a voyage for understanding a problem well enough to be able to come up with a solution that fits a given set of constraints. During the voyage, various aspects of the growing understanding need to be communicated to a diverse set of stakeholders. And this understanding is usually communicated using a mixture of paper and electronic documents. The questions you need to ask in designing this communication are: *What content are you trying to communicate?* and, *What are the most effective media for communicating it?* Failure to address these difficult questions means that people end up with too much, too little, or the wrong information for them to be able to provide necessary feedback.

Do statements like these sound familiar?

- "We have to produce the feasibility report by the end of the week."
- "The functional spec has to be ready by next Tuesday."
- "We have to distribute formal minutes of this meeting to all the stakeholders."

If you reply to these statements by asking why, the answer might be, "Because we have to produce this document at this phase of our project." If you keep probing, and ask, "Precisely what is in the document?

What is it for? Who uses it to make which decisions?" then you discover that people do not know why. They are producing the document because it is the next thing to do.

If you recognize this behavior on your project, you may be working in a paper mill.

In a paper mill, every activity is marked by the production of a document, and progress is measured by how many of the documents have been produced—not by what the documents contain. The paper mill principle says: Just in case anyone needs anything, let's give everybody everything.

Another sign of a paper mill is that the contents of the various documents do not have any formal connection to each other. For example, a process in one document might have a very or slightly different name in another document. So, while people suspect it is the same thing, there is no formal traceability and lots of room for assumptions and confusion. Another indicator of this pattern is that people become obsessed with having documents in their possession. If you produce something—anything—people ask, "Can I have a copy of that?" Everyone wants a copy of everything.

Paper mills are detrimental because when people are focused on the weight of documents that have been produced, they stop thinking about something that is much more important: Are we doing useful work that contributes to the goals of the project?

Projects that are not paper mills use objective measures, agreed upon by the team, such as number of inputs and outputs, business processes, use cases, constraints, features, modules of working code, function points, data elements, or anything else appropriate for the project.[1]

Instead of automatically producing a document, these project teams consider other ways to communicate progress. They use white boards, teleconferences, blogs, and prototypes as communication vehicles. They also discourage the squirreling away of individual documents by keeping project artifacts in a central project library and making them freely available to people who need them.

The point is that every document that is produced should satisfy some well-defined need and should have contents that are traceable to the overall project knowledge.

---

[1]For more information on tailoring the process and the documentation to the project's real needs, see Pattern 12, "System Development Lemming Cycle."

80 Offshore Follies

Dazzled by lower labor rates, the executives launch an offshore development scheme that increases the complexity of communication among development sites.

One of the most reliable ways to elicit a debate among software managers is to bring up the topic of offshore development. Over the past fifteen years, the use of offshore software development and support teams has gone from fringe fad to industry staple, while remaining controversial. Some managers see offshore development as the inevitable path forward, while others see it as a desperate move by clueless cost-cutters. Still others see it as a potentially useful tool that brings with it significant but surmountable challenges. What just about everyone can agree on is that there are many ways for offshore development to go horribly wrong.

Here are a few of our favorite executive epiphanies that doomed the offshore adventures that followed:

- "From now on, when attrition occurs onshore, you will have to hire the replacement person in Franz Josef Land."
- "It looks like we underestimated the amount of work required to complete the portlet component. I hear that

there are three developers in Andorra who are not busy for the next two months. Let's have them help the team here with that."

- "Wow, the schedule for the next release looks really tight. The only way we can get enough developers on it is by going offshore. That will help us finish sooner."

These statements reveal a lack of appreciation for the high cost of inter-site communication and inter-site iteration. Allocating work to sites almost randomly (as attrition occurs, for example) greatly increases the minimum required bandwidth between the sites. Similarly, if the manager from whom a first-line employee receives task assignments and feedback is at another site, the frequency and intensity of communication required between the sites are substantially increased.

The underlying principle here is nothing new. To control the complexity of a system, we have long been taught to partition the system, to minimize the complexity of interfaces among its major sub-components. The same concept applies to the design of work flow in a development team. If the team includes groups of people who are in multiple locations—especially if some are in distant time zones—the stakes are raised considerably. We want to reduce the requirement for frequent, high-bandwidth communication and iteration across oceans. We want to avoid this:

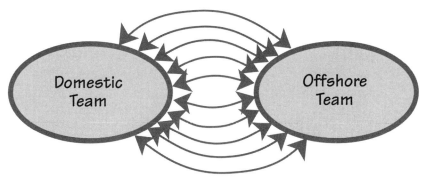

How will you know if you've fallen into an offshore folly? Look for symptoms like these:

- Daily meetings at 6:00 A.M. (or 8:00 P.M.) throughout the development cycle so developers in both locations can sync up with each other.

- Three people onshore trying to manage the work of two developers offshore.
- First-line employees whose direct manager is more than four time zones away.
- An offshore site that does feature development work for six products, but ships nothing itself.

Having said all this, we do not want to discourage you from making use of offshore development resources. We have had success with offshore partners since the early 1990s. To make the most of their potential, consider this advice from the grizzled:

1. Iterate locally. Whenever possible, assign to a single site—either onshore or offshore—phases of the work that require rapid iteration.

2. Recognize that your first few uses of the offshore development model will take longer than they would have if you had done them onshore. Teams need time to develop the new muscles on which successful offshore development relies.

3. Realize that your offshore teams are not different from your onshore teams, in most ways. They want challenging, meaningful work to do. The labor markets in most offshore centers have become extremely competitive. Top software engineers in these markets have choices. They gravitate toward exciting work that gives them an opportunity to advance their skills. They flee from maintenance-only sweatshops.

4. Foster the purpose of each site. Sites need souls. While there are lots of factors that separate healthy sites from unhealthy ones, vibrant sites are usually characterized by a specific mission. They build a specific product or system, or a significant, nameable part of a larger product or system. Conversely, sites that contain many miscellaneous development and support teams with no specific shared purpose often exhibit low energy and low morale. When chartering an offshore development site, think first of how your teams will identify with the site's mission.

These steps, especially the last, can help you avoid *onshore* follies as well.

81 War Rooms

The project is centered through the use of a dedicated war room.

Each year, we come across a scant dozen-or-so projects that have dedicated war rooms, with work products decorating the walls and project members interacting in the project's common space. While this is hardly a major trend, it is a pattern that is worth analyzing, as such projects tend to be hell-bent for success.

> *I'm beginning to think that a project not worth a war room may be a project not worth doing.*
>
> —TDM

The war room is a manifestation of an attitude that a substantial amount of face-to-face interaction is essential to project success. In addition, it asserts that the active display of work products and artifacts is essential to both the jelling of the team and the conduct of its work. Finally, it is clear evidence of someone's willingness to invest aggressively in project success. Real estate is the prototypical form of investment, and a project that is allocated real estate possesses a powerful symbol that it matters.

In most cases, the war room is simply a commandeered conference room. The room is large enough to accommodate any or all of the project team members, with room for a few visitors. Typically, project members are in and around the war room at some time most days, and it is there that they conduct most of the key interface discussions and design and redesign sessions.

Artifacts that are on permanent display include deliverables in progress, the working design, the schedule, PERT and manpower-loading charts, risk lists, work breakdown structure, a mix of work products, and managerial artifacts. Team members gravitate to the war room whenever they're inclined to put their hands on any of the major planning or design artifacts, as well as to view the contributions of their teammates. (There is more on this phenomenon in Pattern 75, "Fridge Door.") In the best cases, individual workers have private work space adjacent to the war room, so that the room and its surroundings constitute a well-defined project domain.

The project manager is a frequent occupant of the war room. It is there that he maintains the pulse of the project. Since some of the artifacts and work products on display are the manager's, analyzing and updating them are war room tasks that naturally accrue to the manager.

The following may be obvious, but it's still worth stating: Just declaring that the project has a war room and setting space aside for it doesn't do the trick. The challenge is to make the war room a vital and organic part of the project. The war room has to emerge as part of the project's own chosen direction; that is the only way the war room is going to be *magical,* as war rooms can sometimes be.

82 What Smell?

People in the organization cannot detect its underlying vitality or decay.

- Madame Fleury's Bakery is in the village of Chamonix in the French Alps. Every morning, each customer who enters to get fresh bread or croissants breaks into an uncontrolled grin; the place just smells so scrumptious. Madame Fleury and her staff give excellent service to their delirious customers, but they are not smiling.

- On the eastern end of Long Island, there are duck farms. Most are family-owned and family-operated. You know you are approaching a duck farm not by seeing it, not by reading a sign for it, but by smelling it. *Stench* is a kind descriptor for the smell. If you can stand to get close enough, your eyes will tear involuntarily. How can the family work on the duck farm, day-in and day-out? The only possible answer is that they just don't smell all those duck deposits.

The metaphorical scent of projects, and of entire organizations, is usually strong; it varies from bakery to duck farm, but the denizens' senses are saturated by the smell.

All workers need to know what their organization smells like, so they can decide to either

- Breathe deeply and do nothing different at all.
- Open the windows a bit.
- Fumigate.

No matter what position you hold in your organization, you cannot determine its smell yourself. You need to bring in some fresh noses from the outside world to sniff around your place. Interestingly, if you have been around projects for a while, you are probably completely capable of doing this task for other organizations. You might be able to set up a Smell-Now: It's-For-Facts (SNIFF) program through a local chapter of a professional society.

We have been sniffing around organizations for years, and without explanation, here are some actual scents we've sniffed, other than bakery and duck farm:

- nursing home
- monkey cage
- teenager's bedroom
- make-up room backstage
- sea breeze
- oncologist's waiting room
- mildew
- playground
- electrical fire
- cigar bar

If you can't guess the kind of organization from its scent, either you're in it, or you have just never walked into that kind of office.

As the Lynyrd Skynyrd lyric goes, "Can't you smell that smell?"

83 Lessons Unlearned

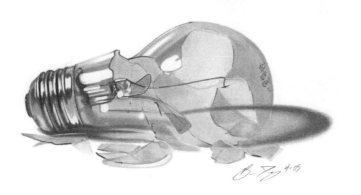

Pencil Drawing by Brian Duey

The team recognizes its mistakes but repeats them anyway.

Which activities are important in your project?

> Writing code? *Definitely!*
>
> Getting the requirements right and testing your product against them? *Oh yes.*
>
> Doing design? *Oh, well.*
>
> Holding Lessons Learned sessions after the project to improve your work methods? *Holding what? Lessons Learned? Why should we waste our time on that? We can't change anything about our last project—it's done. (Finally!) Besides, we don't have time for navel contemplation; the next project is already funded, and we'd better get going.*

If such reactions are common in your company, you're not alone.

One excuse for not examining the project's successes and failures after the fact is a presumed lack of time. Another excuse is more cynical: "What good is it to pore over our past errors? Our company is not going to allow us to change anything anyway. Besides, we have just made it up to CMMI Level 3; we've got to stick to our current approach or we may get sent back to Level 2."

Both excuses are surefire recipes for repeating whatever errors were made the last time around. Failures *that everyone recognizes as failures* find no way to turn around and influence what happens next. So, the same failures happen again.

Just having Lessons Learned sessions at project end is a step in the right direction, but it's not always enough. It's possible to go through the exercise and still not reap the benefit. Consider this exchange:

> "We do these sessions on most projects here. Give the team two hours to reflect on the good and the bad things about the project. They'll feel better after they've vented."
>
> "And then?"
>
> "Um, then everybody moves on to the next project."
>
> "Doing exactly the same things they did before?"
>
> "Well, more or less."

How could this happen? How could the review end up being *primarily* a pressure release mechanism rather than a catalyst for change? The sessions, after all, are justified explicitly as a "mechanism for change." That sounds right, but there's a word missing from that justification: They're actually intended as a "mechanism for *internal* change." And there is the rub.

Projects that conduct after-project reviews often find themselves highlighting problems that are not strictly internal to the project. These problems have root causes in the constraints imposed on the project from the outside: organizational interfaces, inadequate access across political lines, artificial intermediaries, imposed understaffing, early over-staffing, imposed standards that get in the way, crazy schedules, lack of clerical support, and so on. Since the problems are outside the domain of the team, their solutions may be declared off-limits.

While we're at it, changes that lie entirely *inside* the domain of the team are likely to be dauntingly difficult to implement. So, there's the double bind: External change is difficult and scary for political reasons, and internal change is difficult and scary for operational reasons. No wonder the review sometimes turns into a mere gripe session with no serious inclination to change anything.

When a Lessons Learned process ends up being mostly for venting, you'll notice that the published results are observations, not action items. Reversing this phenomenon is mechanically simple, though it may be nontrivial to pull off. The key is to insist on setting action items for identified problems both inside and outside the team's power base: Tie each identification of something that *didn't help or got in the way* to an action item to be applied to the next iteration or release, or on the very next project. This puts the Lessons Learned team in a constructive design mode. Some of the action items will be organizational, but they can't be off the wall. They have to pass the same tests of implementability that their designs of internal project procedures have to pass.

A mechanical trick that is often used to open the sessions is to ask each person to come in armed with at least one good thing and one bad thing to report about the project. (This makes it permissible for participants to raise a subject that otherwise might be thought off-limits.) A similar trick can help close the exercise in a way that will successfully usher in change: Insist that there be at least one action item that lies entirely inside the team's domain and at least one that lies partially or wholly outside.

Each action item should indicate how some method or task or human interface or imposed constraint will be modified the next time around to avoid the problem. The action items have to be explicit, and they have to be directed toward one specific effort—a kind of pilot for the change—where they will be applied. Because the action item limits the requested change to a pilot area, it has more chance of being accepted by outside powers.

Lessons Learned sessions are most often performed at the end of a project,[1] but there are good reasons to conduct interim mini-reviews as well, say, at the end of each iteration or each release.

Companies that benefit from the Lessons Learned exercise are courageous: They allow their approaches and processes and organizational structures to be critically examined—even skewered—and they are truly willing to consider change. Working for this kind of organization can be a joy. The opportunity to catalyze change is something participants find particularly valuable about their company culture.

---

[1] Lessons Learned sessions are also called project retrospectives, postmortems, or post-project reviews. For valuable how-to advice about conducting your own Lessons Learned sessions, see Norman L. Kerth, *Project Retrospectives: A Handbook for Team Reviews* (New York: Dorset House Publishing, 2001).

84 Sanctity of the Half-Baked Idea

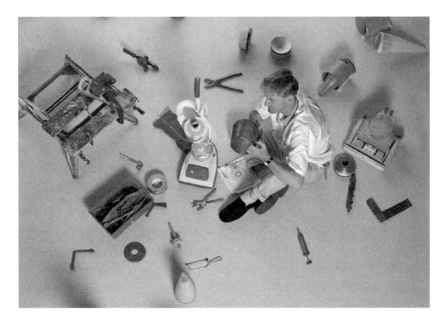

The team is willing to nurture even seemingly half-baked ideas.

Progress can be slowed, and sometimes stopped, when team members are reluctant to offer ideas that appear at first sight to be half-baked. Strong teams make it safe to voice unfinished ideas; many teams encourage this practice. If the idea in its original form is not perfect, it can be improved—but only if it is allowed to have its day in court.

Half-baked ideas play a part in project life and should be thought of as something to be protected and nourished. For example, brainstorming sessions and other creative workshops can only work if team members feel safe to blurt out whatever they come up with, no matter how incomplete, seemingly impossible, or downright harebrained the idea may seem. Further, they can say what's on their mind without fear of personal criticism or ridicule. Experience shows us that even the most half-baked of ideas, when respected and allowed to live, sometimes turn into valuable commercial products.

Allowing half-baked ideas to develop might require a change of behavior. Some people, teams, and for that matter, organizations, have a habit of trashing any idea that is not immediately and obviously viable. Anyone wishing to propose an idea has to think it through, ensure it is watertight, and then propose it in a way that makes its value immediately evident to everybody. With anything less than that, the proposal is a dead duck. By forcing all ideas to be fully formed before they are aired, the organization is denying the benefits of group improvement and choking off what should be a steady stream of project innovations. Most ideas can benefit from having several minds working to improve them.

Humans are better at improving things than they are at inventing things, and almost any idea can be improved—if you keep at it. Understandably, not all team members are great inventors, and not all are as articulate as they would like to be. Tentative ideas are debated—sometimes vigorously—and it is through team discussion that the idea matures and improves. Naturally, not all ideas make it through the debating chamber, but all of them are given a chance.

Ideas are free. Unless time is incredibly short, why rush to discard ideas if they are not immediately viable? All that is needed is also free: a culture in which team members feel able to propose half-baked ideas.

James Dyson's half-baked idea, the centrifugal vacuum cleaner, took 15 years and more than 5,000 prototypes to come to commercial fruition. One Dyson model is now the best-selling vacuum cleaner in the United States, United Kingdom, Ireland, Spain, Belgium, Switzerland, and Australia, and another is the best-seller in Japan.

85 Leakage

Time and money tend to "escape" from closely measured categories into less closely measured categories.

Now here's a dilemma: You're busy perfecting some server-side code to enliven a small piece of the interface to your company's new portal. You've just spent fifteen more hours on the damn thing, and it still isn't right. As you're puzzling over the code, a guy from the Program Management Office stops by, to bug you about your time sheet for the week: "Please log onto the PMO system immediately and fill in the numbers." When you do, you realize that the activity you've been billing your time to for this work, "5321: Implement-Dynamic-Portal-Interface," is almost full. Another fifteen hours will exhaust the time allocated for the task and unleash the inevitable question, "Well, is it done?" Of course it's not done. Frowns all around, and the next question is sure to be, "Well, when will it be done?" Shudder. You don't want to go there.

Fortunately, there is a task on the work breakdown structure with no time yet logged against it: "5977: Tune-For-Response-Time." Now that you look back at what you've been doing for the last fifteen hours (you don't have to look *too* critically), doesn't it seem as much like tuning for response time as implementing a dynamic portal interface?

Sure, close enough. You plunk down the fifteen hours against task 5977. Most task breakdown structures are vague enough to allow for some leeway in how time is reported.

The task that's almost full is being watched closely by management because when its allocated time is exhausted, the work is supposed to be complete. Nobody's got an eye on the other task because it is off beyond mañana.[1] Your innocent little diversion of fifteen hours from one task to the other is what we call *leakage.*

There are two different types of leakage on most projects: either work that is miscategorized when it is done, as in the example above; or work that is partially deferred to a later task. Type 2 leakage is impossible if task descriptions are really tight, but there is usually enough leeway for at least some work to be deferred from early to late tasks. Both leakage types have the same effect: They introduce invisible slip into the project. Either they add work to or remove allocation from late project activities, thus making them harder to complete on-time.

Consider these common examples of leakage:

- Activities whose time or manpower is almost used up are more closely watched than those with remaining allocation, so work leaks from the former to the latter. (This is Type 1 leakage: miscategorization.)
- Activities that are due for completion in the near term are more closely watched than those due at a later date, so some leakage tends to occur, shifting work into the later tasks. (This is Type 2 leakage, since some of the work is deferred.)
- Work leaks out of requirements activities to be handled on-the-fly, as part of coding or testing. (Type 2.)
- Since planned innovation activities tend to be vaguely defined, they sometimes end up as slush buckets. (Type 1, again.)
- Easy work tends to get done before difficult work. This is a form of work leakage from the closely followed meta-category Look How Much We've Already Done to the slightly more amorphous What Remains Left To Do.
- Work leaks out of the project entirely and into the post-project maintenance activity.

---

[1] See Pattern 7, "Mañana."

You might think leakage is purely an accounting matter, of interest only to those who are trying to compile a usable historical profile of project work. But the effect of leakage on the project can be more insidious: It can lead to a partial or sometimes total loss of control. When work leaks out of the project entirely, the result is a shoddy product that needs to be fixed and refixed after delivery; management has thus lost control over product quality. And when difficult work leaks out of early activities (so *they* can be completed on-time), the density of difficulty is increased over time, leading to that old cliché of projects stalled at 95 percent done for a lot more than 5 percent of the time.

> *"Most people understand the time value of money, but not the money value of time."*
>
> —Steve McMenamin

86 Template Zombies

IS THERE SOMETHING WRITTEN IN THIS BOX?

HOW ABOUT THIS ONE?

The project team allows its work to be driven by templates instead of by the thought processes necessary to deliver products.

When you find a project team that is focused on producing a standard document rather than on considering the content of that document, then you are in the land of the template zombies. This obsession with filling in the blanks is characterized by quality checks that work like this:

> "I have finished the Project Initiation Document."
>   "How do you know the document is finished?"
>   "Because I have written something under each one of the headings."
>   "Oh good, now we can get it signed off."

In the land of the template zombies, form takes precedence. It is not necessary to think about the content of the document. It is not really necessary to think at all. The important thing is to have something—anything—under each of the prescribed headings. Not surprisingly, template zombies are adept in the art of cutting and pasting and ignoring anything that does not fit the dictates of the template.

We are not saying that templates are necessarily a bad idea. In fact, they provide a very good way to transmit experience, particularly through checklists and a framework in which to ask questions. The problem occurs when the template becomes fixed in stone and the organization now assumes that every project is a carbon copy of the one that went before it. Template zombies believe that if they put something—anything—in all the boxes on the template, then they are guaranteed success. Rather than facing the awkward reality that every project is different and treating the template as a guide, template zombies succumb to the temptation to put their mind in neutral and fill in the blanks.

> *At one review meeting I attended, team members were discussing a design idea. Someone objected that the template made no provision for capturing that idea. It was supposed to be covered later on, in another document. Rather than changing the template, the team simply rejected the idea.*
>
> *In another organization, the team rebelled. The Powers That Be dictated that the team should use a set of standard templates drawn up by external methodologists. The templates represented one of the worst examples of Paint By Numbers. Adherence to the numbers would have ensured failure. The team members went underground and used approaches that enabled them to get real work done. Then, to satisfy the methodological rules, they engaged a clerk to fill in the fairly meaningless templates. Nobody ever read the resulting documents, but they were considered satisfactory because they contained the required number of pages.*
>
> —SQR

If you find yourself determinedly agonizing over always putting something under each template heading, then chances are that you are being driven by form rather than content and that you are heading toward the template-zombie zone. Similarly, if your development process prevents you from including a model, or anything else that is useful, because it does not fit the template, you may already be in the template-zombie zone. When conversations about the project center on the format, layout, fonts, and numbering systems, then the template zombies are stumbling through the dark toward you.

Photo Credits

Introduction: Copyright © 2007 by Peter Angelo Simon (www.PeterAngeloSimon.com)

Pattern 1, "Adrenaline Junkies": Artwork by Kelley Garner, supplied by iStockPhoto

Pattern 2, "Rattle Yer Dags": Photo © Byron W. Moore, supplied by BigStockPhoto

Pattern 3, "Dead Fish": Copyright © by Stefanie Timmermann/iStockPhoto

Pattern 4, "Happy Clappy Meetings": Photo courtesy of Chris Linn, Corporate Entertainer (www.chrislinn.com) used with permission

Pattern 5, "Nanny": Copyright © by Darryl Mason/iStockPhoto

Pattern 6, "Referred Pain": Copyright © 2005 Tari Faris/iStockPhoto

Pattern 7, "Mañana": Photograph by Mark Lisao (markldxb@gmail.com)

Pattern 8, "Eye Contact": Copyright © 2006 by Leah-Anne Thompson/iStockPhoto

Pattern 9, "Management by Mood Ring": "Mood Ring" by Bruce MacEvoy (www.handprint.com)

Pattern 10, "True Believer": Copyright © by Joseph Jean Rolland Dubé/iStockPhoto

Pattern 11, "Lease Your Soul": Rembrandt's "Faust," from the Wikipedia Commons

Pattern 12, "System Development Lemming Cycle": Photo by llwill/iStockPhoto

Pattern 13, "No Bench": Photographer: gocosmonaut/iStockPhoto

Pattern 14, "Face Time": Copyright © 2007 by Lise Gagne/iStockPhoto

Pattern 15, "I Gave You a Chisel. Why Aren't You Michelangelo?": Copyright: Aleksandr Ugorenkov/iStockPhoto

Pattern 16, "Dashboards": Diagram by James Robertson

Pattern 17, "Endless Huddle": "Academe: Faculty Meeting," burin engraving, 3.9 inches x 6.1 inches (100mm x 155mm), © 2002 Evan Lindquist-VAGA/NY

Pattern 18, "Young Pups and Old Dogs": Photo by Timothy Lister

Pattern 19, "Film Critics": Artist: Dan Leap/iStockPhoto

Pattern 20, "One Throat to Choke": Copyright © Tim Pannell/Corbis

Interlude, "Project-Speak": Copyright © Alexei Garev, used with permission

Pattern 21, "Soviet Style": Copyright © 2007 by Milan Ilnyckyj (sindark.com)

Pattern 22, "Natural Authority": Drawing by Tom DeMarco

Pattern 23, "The Too-Quiet Office": Photographer: Zennie/iStockPhoto

Pattern 24, "The White Line": Photo by David Lee | Agency: Dreamstime.com

Pattern 25, "Silence Gives Consent": Copyright: Karen Squires/iStockPhoto

Pattern 26, "Straw Man": Photo by Suzanne Robertson

Pattern 28, "Time Removes Cards from Your Hand": Photo by Emin Ozkan/iStockPhoto

Pattern 29, "Lewis & Clark": Supplied by Images of American Political History

Pattern 31, "Rhythm": © Nicemonkey | Dreamstime.com

Pattern 32, "The Overtime Predictor": Copyright © by Maciej Laska/iStockPhoto

Pattern 33, "Poker Night": "Card Players" by Pro Hart, used with permission

Pattern 34, "False Quality Gates": Graphic by Kativ/iStockPhoto

Pattern 35, "Testing Before Testing": © Undy | Dreamstime.com

Pattern 36, "Cider House Rules": Copyright © by Bruce Lonngren/iStockPhoto

Pattern 37, "Talk Then Write": Photo by Scott Olson, Copyright © 2007 Getty Images

Pattern 38, "Project Sluts": Copyright: Roberto A. Sanchez/iStockPhoto

Pattern 39, "Atlas": Copyright © by Nick Martucci | Agency: Dreamstime.com

Pattern 40, "Everyone Wears Clothes for a Reason": Copyright © Tim Davis/CORBIS

Pattern 41, "Peer Preview": Copyright © 2007 by Felix Möckel/iStockPhoto

Pattern 42, "Snorkeling and Scuba Diving": "The Atlantic Trench," from the Wikipedia Commons

Pattern 43, "It's Always the Goddamned Interfaces": Copyright © by Frances Twitty/iStockPhoto

Pattern 44, "The Blue Zone": Photographer understood to be John T. Daniels. Library of Congress/Wikipedia Commons

Pattern 45, "News Improvement": From left, (a) Copyright Maartje van Caspel/iStockPhoto; (b) Copyright Guillermo Perales Gonzales/iStockPhoto; (c) Copyright Michael Kemter/iStockPhoto; (d) Copyright Duncan Walker/iStockPhoto

Pattern 46, "Telling the Truth Slowly": "Untitled 12" (2001) by Tai-Shan Schierenberg, courtesy Flowers, London

Pattern 47, "Practicing Endgame": Photo by bluestocking/iStockPhoto

Pattern 48, "The Music Makers": Photo courtesy of Borys Stokowski

Pattern 49, "Journalists": Artist: doodlemachine/iStockPhoto

Pattern 50, "The Empty Chair": Photo by James Robertson

Pattern 51, "My Cousin Vinny": 20TH Century Fox/The Kobal Collection

Pattern 52, "Feature Soup": Artist:Yails/iStockPhoto

Pattern 54, "Ben": Copyright: Pathathai Chungyam/iStockPhoto

Pattern 55, "Miss Manners": Copyright © 2007 by Don Bayley

Pattern 56, "Undivided Attention": Copyright © 2006 by Joanne Green/iStockPhoto

Pattern 57, "There's No Crying in Baseball!": Copyright © 2005 by Rob Friedman

Pattern 58, "Cool Hand Luke": "Confrontation 2" by Chaim Koppelman, Terrain Gallery, used with permission

Pattern 59, "Shipping On-Time, Every Time": Copyright © by eyeidea/iStockPhoto

Pattern 60, "Food++": Copyright © by Sawayasu/iStockPhoto

Pattern 61, "Orphaned Deliverables": Photo copyright © by James Rye

Pattern 62, "Hidden Beauty": Copyright 2007 by Michael Altschul/visuelmedie.dk

Pattern 64, "Children of Lake Wobegon": Photo courtesy of Marja Flick-Buijs, used with permission

Pattern 65, "Co-Education": Copyright: Dmitriy Shironosov/iStockPhoto

Pattern 66, "Seelenverwandtschaft": TOHO / The Kobal Collection

Pattern 67, "Phillips Head": Photo from the Wikipedia Commons

Pattern 68, "Predicting Innovation": Photo by Gabriel Bulla/Stockxpert

Pattern 69, "Marilyn Munster": CBS/MCA/Universal/The Kobal Collection

Interlude, "The Cutting Room Floor": Copyright © by Valerie Loiseleux/iStockPhoto

Pattern 71, "Loud and Clear": Woodcut by Joseph Taylor, Copyright © 2007

Pattern 72, "Safety Valve": Photo kindly supplied by Weir Valves & Controls UK, Ltd.

Pattern 73, "Babel": Supplied by Kunsthistorisches Museum, Wien oder KHM, Vienna

Pattern 74, "Surprise!": Copyright: Pattie Calfy/iStockPhoto

Pattern 75, "Fridge Door": Photo by James Rye/BigStockPhoto

Pattern 76, "The Sun'll Come Out Tomorrow": Photograph by chuwy/iStockPhoto

Pattern 77, "Piling On": Copyright © Radius Images/Alamy

Pattern 78, "Seasons for Change": "Samson and Delilah" woodcut by Bobby Donovan, copyright © 2006

Pattern 79, "Paper Mill": Copyright: Tim Messick/iStockPhoto

Pattern 80, "Offshore Follies": Photo by Peter Hruschka

Pattern 81, "War Rooms": Photo by Peter Hruschka

Pattern 82, "What Smell?": Copyright: Yanik Chauvin/iStockPhoto

Pattern 83, "Lessons Unlearned": Pencil drawing by Brian Duey (www.dueysdrawings.com), Copyright © 2006, used with permission

Pattern 84, "Sanctity of the Half-Baked Idea": Photograph courtesy of James Dyson

Pattern 85, "Leakage": Copyright © by John Carleton | Agency: Dreamstime.com. German image credit: Copyright: Lise Gagne

Pattern Index

1 Adrenaline Junkies...6
39 Atlas 109
73 Babel 200
54 Ben 148
44 The Blue Zone 122
70 Brownie in Motion 192
64 Children of Lake Wobegon 172
36 Cider House Rules 101
65 Co-Education 176
58 Cool Hand Luke..157
27 Counterfeit Urgency 77
Interlude: The Cutting Room Floor.......................................190
16 Dashboards..45
53 Data Qualty 146
3 Dead Fish 12
50 The Empty Chair 138
17 Endless Huddle..49
40 Everyone Wears Clothes for a Reason 112
8 Eye Contact 25
14 Face Time...40
34 False Quality Gates 95
52 Feature Soup 143
19 Film Critics 55
60 Food++ 161
75 Fridge Door 204
4 Happy Clappy Meetings 14
62 Hidden Beauty 166
63 I Don't Know 169
15 I Gave You a Chisel. Why Aren't You
        Michelangelo? 43
43 It's Always the Goddamned Interfaces 120
49 Journalists...136
85 Leakage 230
11 Lease Your Soul..34
83 Lessons Unlearned 225
29 Lewis & Clark...82
71 Loud and Clear..194
9 Management By Mood Ring 28
7 Mañana 22
69 Marilyn Munster 187
55 Miss Manners 150
48 The Music Makers 133
51 My Cousin Vinny 140
5 Nanny 16
22 Natural Authority 66

45 News Improvement...124
13 No Bench 38
80 Offshore Follies..218
20 One Throat to Choke...58
61 Orphaned Deliverables..163
32 The Overtime Predictor 89
79 Paper Mill 216
41 Peer Preview...114
67 Phillips Head...182
77 Piling On...211
33 Poker Night 92
47 Practicing Endgame 130
68 Predicting Innovation 184
38 Project Sluts..107
Interlude: Project-Speak 61
 2 Rattle Yer Dags 9
 6 Referred Pain 19
31 Rhythm 87
72 Safety Valve..197
84 Sanctity of the Half-Baked Idea 228
78 Seasons for Change 213
66 Seelenverwandtschaft 179
59 Shipping On-Time, Every Time 159
30 Short Pencil 85
25 Silence Gives Consent 72
42 Snorkeling and Scuba Diving 117
21 Soviet Style 63
26 Straw Man 74
76 The Sun'll Come Out Tomorrow 207
74 Surprise! 202
12 System Development Lemming Cycle..................................36
37 Talk Then Write..104
46 Telling the Truth Slowly...127
86 Template Zombies...233
35 Testing Before Testing 99
57 "There's No Crying in Baseball!" 155
28 Time Removes Cards from Your Hand 79
23 The Too-Quiet Office 68
10 True Believer 32
56 Undivided Attention...152
81 War Rooms 221
82 What Smell? 223
24 The White Line...69
18 Young Pups and Old Dogs...52

About the Guild

If your organization builds systems of any kind, chances are that some of the methods and approaches that it uses came originally from the Atlantic Systems Guild. The six principals of the Guild are:

Suzanne and James Robertson, the London partners, are the creators of the Volere requirements process, which includes the popular Volere requirements specification template. Their seminars and consulting assignments have helped organizations around the world improve their discovery and communication of requirements. The Robertsons are coauthors of *Mastering the Requirements Process, Requirements-Led Project Management,* and *Complete Systems Analysis.*

Steve McMenamin is vice president of engineering at Borland Software, where he leads development teams building several of Borland's Open Application Lifecycle Management products. Before joining Borland, Steve held executive positions at BEA Systems, Crossgain Corp., and Edison International.

Tim Lister works out of the Guild's New York office. He spends his time helping systems organizations become more effective with what they have. He is a self-proclaimed risk-management zealot who believes that it's all about risk and reward, and that productivity and quality are meaningless unless put into the risk/reward context. Tim is coauthor with Tom DeMarco of *Peopleware* and *Waltzing With Bears.*

Peter Hruschka, based in Aachen, Germany, specializes in requirements and design of embedded real-time systems. He is the codeveloper of the ARC42 template for system architecture documentation. In one of his earlier lives, he pioneered modeling tools for structured and object-oriented methods. He has coauthored half-a-dozen books on methods and tools.

Tom DeMarco is the author or coauthor of twelve books, and a consultant specializing in project success and, sometimes, project failure (litigation). His nontechnical publications include a mainstream novel and a short story collection. He lives in Maine with his wife, Sally O. Smyth.